Ghetto and *Within*

Class, Identity, State and Politics of Mobilisation

Ravi Kumar

AAKAR

In Association with

ŠRUTI

Society for Rural Urban & Tribal Initiative

Ghetto and *Within:* Class, Identity, State and Politics of Mobilisation
Ravi Kumar

First Published, 2010

ISBN 978-93-5002-069-2

Published by
AAKAR BOOKS
28 E Pocket IV, Mayur Vihar Phase I, Delhi-110 091
Phone : 011-2279 5505 Telefax : 011-2279 5641
aakarbooks@gmail.com; www.aakarbooks.com

In association with
SRUTI
Q-1, Hauz Khas Enclave, New Delhi-110 016
Web : www.sruti.org.in
E-mail : sruti@vsnl.com

Printed at
Arpit Printographers, Delhi-110 032
E-mail : arpitprinto@yahoo.com
Ph. : 9350809192

For Martí

Acknowledgement

The present work evolved out of the recent events that characterised the Indian society and polity. I would like to thank Rohit Jain for taking personal interest in the study and facilitating all the logistical support. Praveen Mote has been helpful by constantly reminding me of the deadlines.

This study would have been impossible without the proactive role of the researchers who worked with me on this study, namely Sayeed, Faisal, Mubassir and Vidhi. Fahad has been of great help when it came to translating some of posters in the last hour. He helped me out at a very short notice.

There are people who have always been of great help to me when it came to formulating the study. The discussions with Pratyush and Pothik, my comrades at *Radical Notes*, sharpened my understanding about many of the aspects of identity formation. I would also like to thank Paresh for his help in copyediting and for suggestions about how to express certain nuances in a more organised manner.

My students at the Jamia Millia Islamia have been an important window into the world which I have started to engage with and this work is only an initial impression of that understanding. I owe a lot to them.

Lastly, while I ate into the time that I should have given to Martí and Rama I would thank them for helping me out in so many different ways for letting me complete this manuscript.

Ravi Kumar

Contents

Chapter 1

Context of the Study

A study of the process of ghettoisation acquires relevance when the polity is being defined by identity politics and the politics of class is waning. The primacy of collective identity formation in politics has gained ground with the onslaught of neoliberal politics, laced with the ideas of localisation, difference and autonomy of subjects. Class as a category of analysis has been relegated to the background with a clear intent of marginalising possibilities of resistance to the system. A tendency, which is neither new nor surprising, to sustain the status quo has rejected dialectics as a method and class as the defining category of analysis. This is not to deny the *conjunctural* significance of identity politics insofar as it rips open subterranean repressions and resists the hegemonic powers and discourses. However, an identity politics, which fails to take cognizance of the balance of forces in class terms fails to transcend the systemic logic of repression and gets accommodated in the system.

The study of the ghetto explicated here makes an attempt to understand how certain physical and socio-economic zones within the city space remain outside the purview of contests to transform the essentially unequal social order. In fact, discourses within ghettos, which are defined by the sharing of a common religious identity and which see subjects as victims of an agenda furthered by the state or other segments of society, do not address inequities of various kinds and fail to locate inequality within the production relations that characterise it. Class is never a part of such discourses. These address extends only religion and caste based inequality (see Appendix I) and base themselves in the context of secularism and communalism, which in turn are analysed mostly in terms of their *appearances*, divorced from political economy. In the following pages an effort is made to understand how the idea of a collective develops from within the community as well as in relation to the outside world. It is a complex set which comprises of state, people and politics and which is explored to understand this dynamics which cannot be defined or understood without a context.

Recent times have seen increased polarisation of society on the basis of religion and this has happened despite so-called 'secularism' being the paramount agenda of diverse political formations. Along with this polarisation has come an increased profiling of Muslims as a religious community. The pressure has been so intense that one finds different Muslim groups making efforts to vocalise their 'nationalist' posture (The Hindu, 2007; NDTV, 2008; The Tribune, 2008). The pressure on Muslim community to prove their fidelity towards India was further increased after an extremely vitiated atmosphere was created by a very partisan and anti-Muslim orientation of the media reports (JTSG, 2009; Mander, 2008) on the episodes that took place following the September 2008 bomb blasts in Delhi and then the violence in Mumbai (Kumar, 2008). The general reaction that was fomented, in an otherwise dormant majoritarian ethos of Indian society, consisted of a deep felt sense of doubt regarding nationalist orientation of Muslims and their fidelity towards India as a nation. Particular districts, such as Azamgarh in Uttar Pradesh, were branded as haven for terrorists, and the *profiling*[1] of Muslims got complete as photographs and doubtful narratives of a 'Muslim terrorist' moved from the 'bearded Man' to the sophisticated, English speaking Management or Information Technology graduates as well. The way in which state through its repressive apparatuses and with the effective support of media created a new imagination – where Muslims became the suspicious people – not only enforced the sense of fear and insecurity of a community with much greater vigour but it raised serious questions about the democratic ethos of the state, the idea of equal citizenship as well as the role of identity in determining everyday politics. The Indian State, the 'secular' formations and the Indian intelligentsia, which each day swears by its spurious democratic and progressive ideals lapsed into silence. Reference to these developments becomes necessary to define the *space* and *time* within which this study was carried out. These factors while they strengthened the sense of a collective identity at one level, on another , in a subtle and veiled fashion they negated the possibility of asking

1. Profiling is understood here as a *process* in which individuals or communities are attributed a particular identity. This process rests on the principle of allocating the *profiled* (individuals/communities)with particular characteristics, which are accumulated over a period of time. These attributes are produced by the historical conjunctures, events, narratives and historical-materialist conditions. Gradual additions and modifications are made to the profiles, for instance, media kept telling us after arrests made from Jamia Millia Islamia University following September 2008 bomb blasts or after the arrests of some 'muslim' software professionals in Bombay that we need to get over the traditional construct of a terrorist as someone leading a very conservative, religious life because today even the educated, suave, savy and cosmopolitan individuals can be potential terrorists.

questions about possible divisions of class and caste within.[2] It was amidst all these developments that the researchers went about their task of looking at Jamia Nagar as a possible ghetto and explored its internal dynamics.

The segregation of our society on different grounds is universally recognised and a great deal of literature also points towards stark and ever increasing polarisation on basis of class. Social science in India has been divided over the primary nature of stratification of Indian society – some arguing for caste and others for class. And gender is seen as impinging upon all categories as creating a division between men and women. If one looks at a city, and to my mind Delhi figures as an immediate example, one finds another significant kind of segregation –physical segregation along religious lines. There are areas in the city where a particular religious community dominates, such as Jamia Nagar and its adjoining areas. The identification of this area as belonging to a particular religious community is such that in recent months it has been pointed out that people residing here find it difficult to even access certain basic amenities. The

2. There is constant effort to downplay the issue of division based on caste, for instance, within the Muslim community. The University population represents, primarily, the interests of the ruling elite of a community and Jamia Millia Islamia is no exception. The implementation of OBC reservations despite Supreme Court order is a case in point which demonstrates how the ruling elite among Muslims prefer not to implement any such provision because it would not only be forced to recognise the existence of so many castes within the religion but also have to give away space to an *outside* force, i.e., the State. The whole argument for the minority status of the university emanates from such an understanding and is more of an effort to sustain the hegemony of the elite within the Muslim community over the educational apparatuses.

formation of the city space has been such that one gets today starkly divided habitations based on different religious identities, specifically Muslim and non-Muslim. It also came to light how the majoritarian mental structure does not provide any space to Muslims in its imagination when cases of Muslims being denied houses on rent appeared in media. This is not to suggest that the formation of ghettos can be traced only to the increasing religious polarisation in the city. But this study bases itself on the fact that there is a stark presence of zones of Hindus and Muslims in the city. And through fieldwork it would try to explore the diversity of factors that results in ghetto formation, as well as the political economy of such ghettos.

In order to reflect on the processes that characterise the internal dynamics of an area that appears 'ghettoised' fieldwork was undertaken in the area adjoining the Jamia Millia Islamia in Delhi. This area was chosen because of a kind of religious homogeneity that characterises it and impressions that emanate from this religious homogeneity. It is inhabited by an overwhelming Muslim population, with exceptions of certain patches like *Kaharon ki Gali,* where Hindus stay. While the area has been in the news in the recent past (especially around September 2008) after the controversial killing by the police of two persons alleged to be terrorists, its portrayal in popular imagination has always been as an area which is inhabited solely by Muslims. Even the University, which is in the vicinity, which began as a school way back in 1935 as part of the nationalist movement, despite being a Central University is seen as an institution which caters primarily to one religious community. Misnomers such as the University has reservation for Muslims is something which is commonly found among the people who live outside the university area. Such misnomers, while reflect on the nature of image that the area and the educational institution located within the area transmits it also speaks a great deal about the nature of polarised religious imagination that exists in the city of Delhi. It from such an imagination that the impression of the University as an institution that supports and breeds 'terrorism' gained currency after September 2008 bomb blasts.

The University becomes an important site also to explain how the close relationship that exists between the neighbourhood and the University further contributes to the creation of a collective identity. There is a sense of ownership of the institution involved here, which does not want certain policies to be implemented here or which does not allow certain political orientations to flourish. In other words, this sense of ownership actually embodies particular interests which want to retain the institution as a symbol of a particular community's control and within that community actually the control of its elite. The recent demands for the minority status and how the local community was mobilised in protests and marches tells a great deal about how institutions are also used and made centres for identity based mobilisations. The neighbourhood has an all pervasive presence within the institution. An underlying argument reflected through the different symbols of everyday life also internally reinforce the idea of a close knit community that has a shared problems, political imperatives and cultural nuances. The local neighbourhood appears as an entity that is *externally* seen as representing on form of religious identity, and gets reinforced through the *internal* dynamics of the physical location as well. Inbuilt in this representation of Muslims is their portrayal as *undifferentiated* and *homogeneous* community.

Chapter 2

Secularism, Nationalism and the Problematic of Religious Identity Formation

The neighbourhood in and around Jamia Millia Islamia, therefore, posits two issues to be understood – the emergence of the identity question and hence ghetto formation, how and why it emerges and how is it sustained, and what is the role of identity in furthering class hierarchies. To put it another way, the significance of internal dynamics of a collective identity becomes essential to understand how the collective consolidates and organises itself in the interests of a few.

Due to these portrayals an effort was made to unravel how one can characterise the area (what will be the attributes of such a *ghetto*, if we can term it so) and to see if this *ghetto* is as undifferentiated as is generally argued by the leaders from the community as well as the majoritarian society. Muslims, in India as elsewhere have become the *other*, a community seen with suspicion. Given the contemporary political context, the Muslim question acquired more complexities as scholars expressed concern over the possibility of the very survival of secularism in India (Hasan, 2004). There have been numerous examples of an institutionalised religion based strife fomented by the instruments of state such as police

(Brass, 2004)[3]. The line of argument that looks at this 'deviance' of the state implicitly indicates towards a definition of state that would hold an idea of citizenship based on mutual respect and admiration. This idea has found itself represented in the conceptualisation of 'secularism'. It has been argued by some that the idea of secularism (in the Indian context) has been

> "built on substantial historical foundations, and must be not dismissed, as is being done by many analysts today, as a superficial attempt by a handful of westernised leaders to impose a concept foreign to India" (Hasan, 2004, p. 09).

Inbuilt into such an argument is the perspective of a modern nation state, which separates religion and state, making the latter neutral to any biases. It is in this respect that one finds scholars putting a great amount of faith in the Constitution. Hasan (2004, p. 10) argues that the "the Indian constitutional theory also hopes that development guided by the state, would secularise Indian public life, making these issues less contentious". Chandoke (2004, p. 70) on the other hand, while arguing for "re-presenting" the secular agenda writes that

---

3. Paul Brass writes that "Moreover, it was also now clear enough to me that what have been called Hindu-Muslim riots in India of the past several decades are misnamed, that they could not have been carried out with such force in so many places, in many cases for extended periods of time, and repeatedly, without the complicity of the police and the failure of the political parties in control of government and the administrative and police officers in the districts to prevent riots or at least to contain them once they had begun. In short, what are called Hindu-Muslim riots in India are, in fact, more like pogroms, and have recently, in Gujarat and elsewhere, taken the form of genocidal massacres and local ethnic cleansing as well" (Brass, 2006)

> "secularism has to be cast in a new mode; it has to be located theoretically and practically in the principle of democratic equality. It has to be seen as both, a logical outcome of the principle of democratic equality and as legitimised by the principle of democratic equality. This may fetch the following results, even if a government or group in civil society does not consider itself bound by secularism it is certainly bound by the principle of equality, which is one of the constitutive features of our Constitution".

She argues that the principles/provisions laid down in the Constitution will invoke principle of equality in inter and intra group relationships. This conception of the constitution is based on the idea that the Constitution is the unproblematic body of literature that represents the interests of all segments of population *equally*. Whether this is possible or not is a big question and needs rigorous interrogation. It would also become necessary to unravel issues such as whom does the Constitution represent. At one level, there are possibilities of looking at the legal framework of the state as democratic and egalitarian because state is seen as an institution that represents the unbiased will of the people but at another level it also needs to be emphasised that states at different historical conjunctures have shown different attitude to the issues that confront the majority – the working class and the downtrodden. In other words, the *conjuncturality* of the state, its many instruments, its expressions and the stage (form) of capital accumulation becomes the determining factor of how the state will behave, interpret laws and even modify them to suit the interests of the classes that it represents.

However, the liberal reading of the Constitution fails to contextualise the state as well as individuals and communities in their politico-economic locale. The invocation of the constitution as the *ultimate* authority representing the spirit of secularism fails to explain the disjunct that prevails between the rights enshrined in the constitution and the socio-politico-historico processes that constitute the everyday reality. The apparent division and autonomy of the three structures of legislature, executive and judiciary is nothing more than a farce that tends to generate the idea of a non-partisan system with the rule of capital at its helm. While certain moves of these bodies are used to demonstrate their autonomy no effort is made to look at how in a particular historical time they also seem to act in synchrony. The most relevant example can be the stage/phase of neoliberal capital when the three have worked together to ensure that the savage rule of capital persists and have shown clearly how the interests of labour will remain subservient to that of capital. It is this subservience of labour to capital which also constitutes the framework of Constitution, which is designed to safeguard private property and, therefore, fails to radicalise the conception of equality which could challenge its very basis. The obvious instances of how interests of *some* are safeguarded against that of the *majority* are judgments that drive out poor from the city confines (the cases of lakhs of slum dwellers being driven out from Yamuna Pushta, Nehru Place, Alaknanda etc.,). The idea that there can be an autonomous institution that would safeguard the interests of the sufferers is misplaced because the judiciary becomes an institution that *interprets*. Hence, while one finds judgments on right to education that ask state to read this right in conjunction with Right to Life there are other judgements that ask the state not to interfere in the fee structure or determination of admission policies of private institutions. There have been occasions where the law has taken a position against removal of illegal shops from Delhi roads but has strongly recommended eviction of slum dwellers. There are many more examples of how the law is interpreted in different ways to suit the needs of times (read it as 'need of capital'). It also becomes an instrument that convolutes the principle of democracy and equality through blurring the complexities that characterise sections of society (as evident in Right to Education Bill or Forest Rights Act).

The contextuality of Constitutional provisions is very important. Unless this contextuality, or the *conjunctural* relationship between the instruments of state and political economy is located it is difficult to understand how the constitutional framework or the different instruments of state are constituted. Only then can one explain why and how a state becomes partisan and takes to right-wing fundamentalism negating the idea of equal citizenship. The relationship between individuals of two different communities is not only made of some abstract notion of admiration and respect for each other but their relationship is also grounded in some form of concrete material reality.

Neither the constitutional framework nor the instruments of are static. Their characters do not exist in autonomy, but are derived from their *state of being* which is contingent upon the needs of capital. It is the requirements of capital which determine the nature of the legal framework that governs a society.[4] Law, therefore, has its own function for the larger system."...it tends to create a social conformism which is useful to the ruling group's line of development" (Gramsci, 2004, p. 195). Gramsci sees it as an organ of political hegemony (ibid, p. 246). Discussing the purpose of law he says that

> "If every State tends to create and maintain a certain type of civilization and of citizen (and hence collective life and of individual relations), and to eliminate certain customs and attitudes and to disseminate others, then the Law will be its instrument for this purpose (together with the school

4. There are, no doubt, instances of provisions getting included due to massive pressure of popular movements. But at the end of it, such insertions in the Constitution do not really endanger the existence of capitalism.

> system, and other institutions and activities). It must be developed so that it is suitable for such a purpose – so that it is maximally effective and productive of positive results" (Gramsci, 2004, p. 247).

He argues that the superstructure of a society is not autonomous and is never left to develop on its own though the focus may appear to be the economy.

> "Because one is acting essentially on economic forces, reorganizing and developing the apparatus of economic production, creating a new structure, the conclusion must not be drawn that superstructural factors should be left to themselves, to develop spontaneously, to a haphazard and sporadic germination. The State, in this field, too, is an instrument of "rationalization", of acceleration and of Taylorisation. It operates according to a plan, urges, incites, solicits, and "punishes", for, once the conditions are created in which a certain way of life is "possible", then "criminal action or omission" must have a punitive sanction, with moral implications, and not merely be judged generically as "dangerous". The Law is repressive and negative aspect of the entire positive, civilizing activity undertaken by the State" (Gramsci, 2004, p. 247).

In a sense, Law like any other instrument of state serves the twin purpose of being an Ideological State Apparatus as well as a Repressive State Apparatus creating consensus as well as being coercive whenever required. While, it is part of a discourse that tends to create conformity with the system, it is also invoked when non-conformist tendencies threaten the existence of the state. In other words, legal frameworks, constitutional theories or the practice of the legal system cannot be extracted out of their location in the social structure, which provides them their particular interpretive colour and makes them instruments of state. For instance, "a large body of research on the role of courts and adjudication... documented the gap between the promises of fairness and equality and the practices of the legal process" (Seron and Munger, 1996, p. 191), establishing that law cannot be free from its own biases and, therefore, cannot be assumed to tackle the issues of inequality and marginalisation in society. It needs to be recognised that "the system of justice is thoroughly embedded in the class structure" (Seron and Munger, 1996, p. 192). This argument also derives its strength from an assertion which was made by Marx when he argued (without emphasising the possibility of hierarchisation of base and superstructure)[5] that

> "In the social production of their life, men enter into definite relations that are indispensable and independent of their will, relations of production which correspond to a definite stage of development of their material productive forces. The sum total of these relations of production constitutes

---

5. In fact, it needs to be mentioned here that the significance of superstructure in determining the nature of base was acknowledged very clearly by Engels in a letter to J. Bloch in 1890:

   "...According to the materialist conception of history, the *ultimately* determining element in history is the production and reproduction of real life. More than this neither Marx nor I have ever asserted. Hence if somebody twists this into saying that the economic element is the *only* determining one, he transforms that proposition into a meaningless, abstract, senseless phrase. The economic situation is the basis, but the various elements of the superstructure – political forms of the class struggle and its results to wit: constitutions established by the victorious class after a successful battle, etc., juridical forms, and even the reflexes of all these actual struggles in the brains of the participants, political, juristic, philosophical theories, religious views and their further development into systems of dogmas – also exercise their influence upon the course of the historical struggles and I many cases preponderate in determining their *form*... (Engels, 1977, p. 487) (emphasis original)

> the economic structure of society, the real foundation, on which rises a legal and political superstructure and to which correspond definite forms of social consciousness" (Marx, 1977, p. 503).

The above statement by Marx also argues that there is a *conjunctural* relationship between the legal and other superstructural forms and the stage of capitalist development. This relationship is defined by the needs of capital, the State being its agent. The politics of the State is defined through this relationship, and this makes the possibility of the State being partisan and biased towards certain groups, communities and classes amply clear. Does this also challenge the idea that the State and its instruments become repository of secular values and ideas?

This brings us to the very contentious issue of how should one understand secularism. Scholars have debated this extensively. Some of them go to the extent of arguing that the very notion of secularism "...in South Asia as a generally shared credo of life impossible, as a basis for state action impracticable, and as a blueprint for the foreseeable impotent" (Madan, 1987, p. 748). It is not only seen as alien to Indian ethos but is even called a myth.

> "Secularism is the dream of a minority which wants to shape the majority in its own image, which wants to impose its will upon history but lacks the power to do so under a democratically organised polity. In an open society the state will reflect the character of the society. Secularism therefore is a social myth which draws a cover over the failure of this minority to separate politics from religion in this society in which its members live. From the point of view of the majority, "secularism" is a vacuous word, a phantom concept, for such people do not know whether it is desirable to privatise religion, and if it, how this may be done... For the secularist minority to stigmatise the majority as primordially oriented and to preach secularism to the latter

> as the law of human existence is moral arrogance and worse – I say "worse" since in our times politics takes precedence over ethics – political folly" (Madan, 1987, pp. 748-749).

Madan's argument is that religion has been an intrinsic part of Indian lives. Gandhi remarked that politics and religion cannot be seen as separate. However there are scholars who have countered such analysis. For instance, Pantham argues that

> "the critics of Indian secularism seem to me to be mis-describing the Gandhian perspective either as a premodern, preliberal, antisecular approach to religious tolerance...or as a traditional peasant-communal moralism that has been re-done either for subserving the bourgeois-liberal project of modernity in India ...or for promoting communalism among both Hindus and Muslims (...). Against these interpretations, I am suggesting that Gandhi pioneered a way of moral-political experimentation in which the relative autonomy (or, in other words, the nonabsolute separation) of religion and politics from each other is used for the reconstruction of both the religious traditions and the modern state" (Pantham, 1997, p. 540).

The discourse of secularism in India is manifested in two different kinds of works: (1) there is one kind of work that looks at the conceptual genealogy of secularism in the history politics and society of the country; and (2) there is another kind of work which emerges primarily as a response to the 'communalisation' of the state society and history. Sociologists such as T N Madan make efforts to understand the first category whereas there are many social scientists (and such work has multiplied tremendously in the recent past, ever since the ascendance of the right wing Bharatiya Janata Party) who have produced their analysis falling into the seond category mentioned above. While scholars have tried to interrogate the very notion of secularism and its relevance to the Indian situation, some have proceeded with the presumption that a modern nation state that was created post-independence implied a secular ethos. Hence, their concerns range from the violence that happens between different religious groups to the possibility of deviations that may crop up within the instruments of state due to different reasons. Efforts to problematise the State and class politics are always lacking in such endeavours.

The most obvious concern for burgeoning literature on the issue during last two decades has been the emergence of a right wing fascist offensive in the country. This offensive further sharpened the identitarian politics based on religion. Such identities have existed for quite long as has been highlighted by some of the scholars (Joshi and Josh, 1992).[6] However, there are others who argue that people's identities along religious lines were not clearly demarcated in the pre-colonial times and collectives were organised largely according to caste, region and language (Pandey, 1990). Hence, the Muslim-Hindu divide is largely a colonial construct. There have been examples of how purely class based peasant riots during 1919 or during 1940s were given religious overtones. Pandey shows how economic conflicts involved the Hindu and Muslim zamindars and the Kurmi, Koeris poor peasants during 1920s in Eastern Uttar Pradesh. However, the British reported it as a religious riot. Such portrayals happen even today when the political economic aspects of riots/conflicts are suppressed and they are shown as conflicts between two different religious communities. Nevertheless, it does not mean that the problem lies with interpretation and historiography only. While the British pursued their own agenda of Divide and Rule, many small

6. Saberwal narrates incidents of how even way back in the 1960s a 'bar of separation' between Hindus and Muslims existed and speaks of how it "has been hardening since the late nineteenth century" (2004, p. 94).

associations and organisations came into being such as the Hindu Mahasabha, Arya Samaaj, and Rashtriya Swamsevak Sangh. Religious identities were being given a shape that would later on, on several occasions, express itself violently.

Post-independence, in the early phases the Congress tried very hard to maintain peace and harmony and right wing political formations were relatively quiet till 1960 or so. Even as the Congress had pretensions of being a pro-Muslim political formation, it also housed some hardcore traditionalists within its fold (Jaffrelot, 1999). The decade of 1960-70 was the phase of organisational building and strengthening of right wing formations in India. In the 1960s the violent face of right wing ideology was visible in form of M S Golwalkar, the RSS leader whose initiative led to the formation of Vishwa Hindu Parishad (VHP) in August 1964. Very soon regional chauvinism among Maharashtrians was evoked by the formation of Shiv Sena, which not only engaged in violence against South Indians (and in due course against people from Bihar and Uttar Pradesh) but also played a significant role in attacks on Communist Parties and Left affiliated Trade Unions (Gupta, 1982). In other words, while the rhetoric of Hinduism and of regional chauvinism was providing mobilisational ground to right wing assertion their class politics was also becoming amply clear.

Ahmad explicates this phenomenon in a *conjunctural* manner. While arguing that "the RSS has demonstrated an astonishing pattern of calibrated growth since its inception in the late 1920s" (1996, p. 281) he shows how its steep ascendance in the 1970s happened "with its participation in the anti-Indira agitations spearheaded by Jaiprakash Narayan and its subsequent inclusion in the Janata cabinet" (pp. 81-82). The Sangh became a respectable name in national politics. This was also a phase of crisis when "the Congress model of capitalist accumulation had exhausted its potential" (1996, p. 282), *garibi hatao* being one of the last vestiges of the populist effort to mobilise people with slogans of redistributive justice. What the Congress was banking on for popular mobilisations was the legacy of the nationalist movement with its "dynamic model of embourgeoisment" that promised "some redistributive justice as well as benefits of rapid rise in incomes for substantial sections of the population, especially at the middling levels of class formation" (Ahmad, 1996, p. 284), and which effectively tackled the challenges from the Left as well as the Right. But this legacy was exhausting itself by the end of the 1960s.

> "In short, it was the collapse of a Left-liberal kind of nationalism that provided the major opening for a fascist kind of nationalism, which set out, both to exploit the weaknesses of that earlier nationalism as well as to formulate a different national agenda" (Ahmad, 1996, p. 285).

The rise of the Sangh Parivar in the political horizon of India implied many things, including the construction of the idea of the 'other' in terms of religion This idea of the 'other' later on defined the hatred of the Hindu right wing towards Muslims and Christians. Elaborated in detail by M S Golwalkar, this hatred based itself on the twin definitions of homeland – *pitribhumi* (fatherland) and *punyabhumi* (spiritual homeland).

> "Being born an Indian is thus not enough to qualify for true citizenship because 'India' designates only a territory; the *Spirit* of India reside, generally, I religions that arose within Indian and, quintessentially, in Hinduism, so that to be a true Indian one had to be a Hindu as well; hence the insistence on the essential identity of territory with religion, and of religion with nation. In other words, Hindus were true citizens of India *prima facie* by having spontaneous recourse to that national Spirit by the fact of birth in a Hindu household, but non-Hindus *could* become citizens by acquiring – that is to say, submitting to – that Spirit – not as *equal* citizens, since nothing could compensate for the taint

> of inferior birth, but as protected minority, or as wards of the state as it were" (Ahmad, 1996, p. 275). (Emphasis original)

With this kind of ideological narrative guiding the political project of the right wing in India, the tendencies of collective identity formation among other religious groups out of fear appeared as a natural outcome. It has been argued by some that the nature of the organisations working under the umbrella of the Parivar (literally meaning 'family') has been fascist.[7]

> "In its staging of spectacles, in its techniques of mobilisation in the multiplicity of its fronts, in the shadowy traffic between its parliamentary and nonparliamentary organs, in the seamless interplay of form and content in its ideological interpellations, in the connection it asserts between a resurgent national tradition and the regaining of masculinist virility, in its simultaneous claims to legality and extra-legality, in its construction of a mythic history which authorises it to be above the civil parliament whenever it so chooses, the Sangh parivar is a classically Fascist force - with large Indian twists of course, as every fascism must always take a specifically national form" (Ahmad, 1996, p. 273).

This brings us to the very pertinent question of how there have been under currents inside the Indian polity which have created the 'other' of people living within Indian society. This 'other' has been created, 'historically speaking', through a process that started with the efforts of the British administration and Indian revivalists. It would be fallacious

---

7. Ahmad writes that there is no possibility of a fascist rule on the horizon, neither is communalism as such fascism but the event of the destruction of the Babri Masjid and the forces which carried it out are definitely fascist in character (1996, p. 270).

to argue that Congress has had a perfect 'secular'[8] record. Implicit in such an argument would be the denial of the *conjunctural* significance of the economy and politics to the agenda of secularism and the character of State. Opposition to secularism from fundamentalist religious groups of different hues and colours has not occurred for the sake of some *apparent* issues but in *essence* they have been reflections of class struggle.

The Indian polity which saw latent forms of religious sectarianism that defined the Muslims as the 'other' earlier has seen an overt emergence of right wing fascistic tendencies since Independence. The 'other' became a victim of hatred on many occasions but this has largely been a result of reasons that are not purely religious. Religion becomes an identity around which the ideological apparatuses weave a web of justifications for their own mobilisation. Historians have argued how "ideological and political struggle for transforming existing consciousness or mediating between narrow economic struggles and the wider social and political struggle was also necessary if economic struggles were not to degenerate into communal and caste warfare, especially in situations where the immediate local enemy could be identified in terms of his separate caste or religious identity" (Mukherjee, 1988, p. 2179). This happened in the case of the Malabar revolt of 1921 as well as in Bengal and Punjab during 1947. Breman (2002, 1993) shows with examples from Gujarat how the lumpenisation of the labour force results in building up of army of rioters on occasions apart from the gradual formation of ghettos within the cities.

---

8. In fact, many have argued that the state is neither secular nor communal. It uses the instrumentalities of secularism and of communalism as and when required by capital for the salvation and sustenance of its hegemony.

Chapter 3

Identity Formation and the Class Question

We have seen above how collective identities get constituted not through some *a priori* and *given* factors but they are based in the actual, concrete material conditions where the individuals who constitute the collective are located. Times of crisis only make the situation more volatile and formation of identities easier. Otherwise there are primarily two ways through which collective identities get constituted. On the one hand there are *external* factors (external to the individual but located within it as well) which create a situation which compels a group to constitute itself into a collective identity. An example can be religion based violence encouraged by the emergence of the right wing in India. It is *external* only in the sense that a situation is created which is outside of the group/community but it is also *internal* because such a situation would not arise unless the possibility of the 'other' is there. In other words, if the right wing hatred wants to construct the 'other' a religious or regional group as the 'enemy', as someone who has 'different' and 'opposed' attributes, has to be created. This enemy is more a 'social' construct, which is devoid of its economic content. It is only 'social', in the sense that it is either religious or regional. It is ignored that they are located in concrete material conditions and have particular attributes which arise from those concrete conditions. Such a construction of the social 'other' allows the politics of capital to successfully push back the actual (which is the 'essence') realities of everyday struggles and conflicts determined by unequal social relations.

If we take the example of Muslims, the fact that there is a fear, a danger waiting outside of their locality, becomes the *external* factor that necessitates the creation of a collective as a safeguard. Once, this sense of an external threat gains ground, the internal dynamics of the collective comes into play and uses different symbols (some of which may be used even by external elements) to strengthen the feeling of oneness, homogeneity and unity. The two groups become the 'other' for each other, each blaming the other for its miseries. While this identity formation is in process, the discourses woven around it, and inside it, seldom make an effort to relate it to the larger systemic problem which facilitates the formation of such an identitarian politics. Rather the question of identity becomes a cultural question, which is not seen as "conditioned/shaped by material forces and social relations linked to production". No doubt the unravelling of the differences which have been "historically denigrated" "have helped uncover the genealogy of terror hidden within the drama of Western democratic life" (Sactamburlo-D'Annibale and McLaren, 2003, p. 152).

Martha Gimenez stresses the centrality of class within the Identity question in a slightly different way when she argues that

> "politics, as ideology (e.g. multiculturalism, diversity) and as practice, obscures how class location is the source of common experiences and problems, opening and closing educational, social and economic opportunities. Such commonalities transcend racial, ethnic and cultural differences and could be the base for collective mobilization and organizing in a variety of settings, such as neighborhoods, schools, communities, and workplaces" (Gimenez, 2006, pp. 431-432).

If one looks at the discourse as it unfolded post globalisation one encounters the primacy of identities other than class as fundamental categories of analysis. The miseries of people, their deprivation and marginality are addressed more as consequences of their cultural or social identities that were suppressed by hegemonic identities. While it may be true that certain communities in specific circumstances have been victims of repression, but what one tends to forget (or intentionally ignore) is that their repression emerged out of a certain kind of class politics that pushed them to marginality in order to sustain its own class hegemony. And it is also important, therefore, to look at how class politics operates within what is described as a homogeneous identity. *Identity becomes an ideological apparatus in the service of the hegemonic class.*

Gimenez furthers her argument by saying that

> "the ideological 'subject effect'; i.e. the transformation of human beings into subjects – both in the sense of self-determining individuals and persons subjected to class and other forms of domination – is both a barrier to the closing of the gap between class and identity politics and, at the same time, a means through which the gap could be closed, through the rethinking of identity as grounded in both difference and commonality, a unity of opposites in which the ability to see oneself as an object of historical, global forces and national class dynamics is the first step to becoming part of the collective Subject of history. To remain bound to identity politics is to accept the terms of those who, ..., use race (and ethnicity) as markers of class while leaving class out of the bounds of political discourse" (Gimenez, 2006, pp. 436-437)

In other words, how one understands the constitution of identities becomes a vital question to understand class politics, which is furthered through a well crafted discourse that derives strength from the ideas that celebrate localisation and individuation and a fragmented world view, in which the dialectics of parts amongst themselves as well as with the larger system remains conspicuously absent. Chandra sees the emergence of identities as a natural consequence of the ethics of capitalist development.

> "The present socio-economic structure, rightly termed an 'acquisitive society', derives its dynamic energy from the competitive engine inherent in the logic of capital accumulation. Wherever it has penetrated, capitalism has appropriated the pre-existing social structures and metamorphosed them, radically transforming their basic structures and converting them into ideological 'instruments', while more or less retaining their form. This process embeds the universal in particular. On the one hand, competition becomes more and more general, as 'non-capitalist' structures are penetrated; on the other hand, greater competition increases social fragmentation, creating multiple new hierarchical identities within society. This is why globalization and postmodernity go hand in hand" (Chandra, 2003, p. 139).

Ahmad, on the other hand argues that

> "Indeed, the proliferation of linguistic, regional, denominational or caste-based identities, combined with the extremities of class polarisation in a backward capitalist society, serve only to *accentuate* the objective need for strengthening of a national identity corresponding to the exigencies of the national market and the nation state, if that market and that state are to reproduce themselves over an extended period of time" (Ahmad, 1996, p. 288).

While trying to understand this phenomenon it is generally forgotten how cultural aspects assume significance in the formation of such identities. Despite the dire economic condition and impoverishment of the vast mass within it, the Muslim leadership has not been able to take up the grievances of unemployment, land reforms, informalisation of the labour force etc. The organisation of the community has seldom been around these issues except when efforts were made by the Left. Hence, some have argued that "it is only cultural grievances, both real and imaginary, that seem to psychologically move the Muslims" (Sonalkar, 1993, p. 1346). A sense of deprivation has always been attributed to them. The arguments of how they have been deprived and discriminated by the state have also cropped up.

In fact, the idea of *discrimination* and *deprivation* (also emerging out of discrimination) constitute the core of the arguments constructed to build up an identity politics. The discourse which seeks to define and understand the problem of Muslims looks at the idea of discrimination as taking place at the hands of an externally present community. In fact, this also brings us to the interesting idea of how internal cohesion is created by attributing the reasons for all ills onto an external agency. The internal dynamics of the community is ignored, the interplay of classes within the community (and, therefore, community is treated as an overarching phenomenon) get ignored. This is also, implicitly, a rejection of the idea of deprivation that happens as a result of exploitative social relations within the community. This has been a problem central in the formation of collective identities and the celebration of these identities as a medium of empowerment.

The political situation that has come about in the last few decades has provided propitious conditions for formation of an overarching Muslim identity. In this process of identity formation the role of the state, apart from the above discussed offensive by the right wing political formations, has been determining. The discourse of the Indian State on terrorism, and the way this discourse is now embedded in our everyday lives has furthered concretisation of this identitarian existence. This approach of the state in post Partition days not only shaped the immediate sense of being the 'other' among Muslims but also left a deep scar in their memories. While works on Partition by scholars such as

Pandey (1997, 2001) help us understand how the Partition episode may have helped create identities along religious lines, works by Robinson (2005) and Chatterji and Mehta (2007) reflect on the construction of identities as embedded in the everyday lives of Muslims who have been victims of religious strife in recent times. A look at history reveals a constant reminder to the Muslims, a refreshing of their memory, about how they remain the 'other' for society.

It is in this context that the significance of memories becomes instrumental in determining the identity of the self and of the community as a whole. While memories of individuals, grounded in a particular context as poor, rich or as placed in a particular region, become sources of knowing and understanding the self within the larger world, they also become instruments for the elite within the community to mobilise and tie the masses into one monolithic community by invoking the memories of victimhood. Memories of violence, in this sense, have one such lasting effect. This is not to discount the significance of memories for the self or the individual. It is only to suggest that there is a constant interplay happening between the self, as a victim of violence, and the constitution of the collective through the medium of violent past of the selves and individuals. So, even as memories are mediated through the context of the self, they also constitute the context. The memories of Partition or for that matter religious violence become important determinants that define one's identity and location in the world. Pandey points out how the Partition of India can be understood in two different ways

> "The two faces of the Partition and Independence of India in 1947 are not in fact, I want to suggest, two separate faces at all - for the two condition each other, constitute each other, at every step. If there are two faces in evidence in northern India at this time, they are the faces of different classes - which I shall call, loosely, a 'ruling (privileged) class'

> celebrating Independence, and a 'refugee class' unable to do so (Pandey, 1997, p. 2262).

In the memory of a victim of Partition it is not only the 'other' community which becomes responsible for his/her plight but the state which failed to do much for them is also responsible. The violence that marked the Partition days, and the partisan role played by the then Indian state, constituted these communities the way they are today. After Partition, for instance, according to Pandey the Meo peasants, in and around Bharatpur, Alwar etc., who converted to Islam centuries earlier and always "had always worn its Islam lightly" (1997, p. 2264) became 'Muslim' and therefore 'Pakistani'. With state's partisanship matters became worse... The legacy of the Partition days seem to linger on as this partisanship of the state, as highlighted in this paper, even in contemporary India, has played a considerable role in determining the nature of identity formation among these communities. The following episode is revealing in nature in this context

> "It was after Gandhi had visited the Purana Qila camp on September 13, 1947 that the Indian government sent out the message clearly that these camps of Muslim refugees were also 'our' camps, and these refugees 'our' citizens if they wished to stay - fully the responsibility of the government of India. And it was after this, it seems, that Indian officials took over full responsibility for the supply of rations as well as for security at these camps. It is a telling comment on the place assigned to the Muslims in the early days of independent India" (Pandey, 1997, p. 2265).

The inhumanity of the state raises aspersions on its 'secular' credentials and therefore once again compels us to ask whether 'secularism' is as simple as a 'a way of life' embedded in the idea of hierarchised and dominant-dominated paradigm of 'tolerance' (Kumar, 2004). In fact, experiences of violence of these communities have determined their social, economic, political and cultural location in the milieu of which they are a part.

> "Violence and community constitute each other, as it were. It is important to reiterate, however, that they do so in many different ways; that slippages occur in the very accounts that signal such a mutual constitution; and that the communities thus constructed are necessarily fragile and open to question, however much they come to be invoked in the social and political turbulence" (Pandey, 2001, p. 188).

Communities have reconstructed themselves after being deprived of their sense of belonging and of being at home. Similar experiences were a result of the Partition of Bengal. How these communities recreate this sense of being at home, belonging and of a new location within which they find themselves creates a newer identity. The way the Bengalis from Bangladesh came and settled in different parts of North India, and the whole dynamics that was set in motion by their settlements provided them an identity with different meanings in different locations, such as in West Bengal or Uttar Pradesh. However, these identities may also evaporate over generations as with changing times and spatial locations, notions of belonging and communities also change.

When newspapers read that 'a terrorist need not always be a conservative looking Muslim but can be a smart looking, information technology savy, urbane person who has been living in your vicissitudes, they are not only re-creating a profile/identity of a community but are also acting in a way to redefine how the individual selves would read their own existence in the new situation. After the Batla house episode my friends living in Delhi would not stop asking me how we were producing terrorists in the University. A general sense of distrust towards Muslims is built up every time an incident of this kind takes place. The media acts overtime to create such a discourse as was evident recently in and around Jamia. It has been a well documented fact the way physical spaces in India get defined according to religion. For instance, "every city has its 'Pakistan' and within each neighbourhood, boundaries innocuous of other, designate 'India' from 'Pakistan'" (Robinson, 2005, p. 50)

The images created by the media or the discourses set in motion by different factors do not happen in abstraction but have a profound basis to it. The images or the appearances need to be transcended to develop an understanding of objects and subjects that concern us. Al-Azmeh (2003) tells us that "we have to curb our fascination with the imposing visibility of things Islamic and the political stakes associated with them. Fascination is none other than beholding an object as if it were a marvel, and the spectacle of marvels suspends the normal operation of human understanding" (p. 36). Unless the human understanding is shaped through these cautions it will be difficult to look at the "vast industry of misrecognition" that has been put in place "as much by advocates of Islamism" as by others "purporting to find, over and above the complex and multiple histories and present conditions of Muslim peoples, a homogeneous and timeless Islam, constructed as a culture beyond society and history, a repository of 'meaning'" (ibid, p. 36). This flawed understanding furthers creation of a collective identity not only through the variables that are present *outside* (or are *external* to the community) but also through forces that are very much active *inside* (or the *internal* factors) the community, which is sharply divided across class and caste lines.

The symbols which define the identity of the collective, such as posters, try to convey an image of the Muslims as a homogeneous collective. A look at the posters and graffiti in the area brings out some very revealing facts about politics and public discussions in the area. All posters put up by religious organisations try to portray the community as united and driven towards a common goal. Though various Islamic sects and their national offices exist in this area, the differences among them don't come out in the open discourse of posters, graffiti and public speeches. None of them argue exclusively for their sect's ideology. Jamaat-e-Islami Hind, which pastes posters for its weekly meetings, also takes up common issues of concern to all Muslims as topics of discussions. Names of prominent Muslim leaders are invoked by each of these organisations to give an impression that the organisation addresses concerns of the Muslim community as a whole and a reflection of it can be seen in the some of the posters calling for 'Muslim political awakening', in which three fourth part of the poster carries names of different prominent Muslim personalities from all walks of life. With over 40 names the poster is more a show-off of a united Muslim front than any specific demand or message. The poster was put up by the All India Milli Council which has been trying to act as an umbrella for Muslim organisations. In order to broaden the base and as an effort to reach out to the wider mass with the kind of messages it would like to convey the organisation posters have names of Shia, Sunni as well as Sikhs.

Some posters from the Joint Committee of Muslims for Empowerment came up, highlighting issues like reservation for Muslims and other 'community' issues. Interestingly this committee which claims to be a joint committee had names of a very few Muslim organisations, most of which are puritan.[9]

---

9. Puritan thought in Islam believes that local Islam/lived traditions got contaminated in India by coming in touch with other traditions. Therefore, purification of religion is necessary by basing it on what the religious texts taught. Puritanism in the area is related with 'cultural capital' as, it was equated with education. Most of the educated respondents said that Barelviat is due to ignorance. Many people who actually belong to 'barelviat' tried to hide their identity. '*Yeh jahiliyat ki wajah se hai. Padh likh ke log samajhdar*

The poster also had the name of Popular Front of India (PFI), an organisation from South India, which, further more, is constituted by three other organisations — Karnataka Forum for Dignity (KFD) from Karnataka, National Development Front (NDF) from Kerala and MMK from Tamilnadu. These Muslim organisations came up together after communal flare ups, and are know to take militant positions with communal overtones. The National Development Front in Kerala particularly is opposed by many Muslim organisations for being explicitly communal.

---

ho jate hain", ('this is due to ignorance, people become intelligent after studying') said one respondent. In a certain sense the presence of Puritanism was also quite evident.

People even say that the emerging base of the RSS in Kerala is due to NDF activities. Our fieldwork reveals its communal character.

All the prominent religious organisations, Jamaat-e-islami Hind, Jameat ulma-ẹ-Hind, Ahl-e Hadis etc., speak up on political issues; the issue of Israel's oppression on the Palestinians is one of the most commonly discussed issues. Such issues allow construction of an image of Muslims as victims because of their religious identity, all across the globe. This has become an issue for mobilisation especially since 9/11 and the witch hunting of Muslims that has been happening across the globe since then. These posters are full of heavy words to evoke 'Muslim' emotions. One poster even used striking images to make the appeal stronger.

These posters use very sentimental words to describe how Muslims are being targeted like — 'Operation Batla House', 'blood lusty terrorism' and so on.

All the political posters except those of the Congress communicate a sense of victimhood to the Muslim

community. Congress posters incidentally don't talk about these issues. They talk about leaders and their capacity to 'lead', specially lead towards a 'secular' India. They want to redefine religion, and to talk about these issues they use the words like "dharma" (religion). It indicates how the politics of the Congress is also closely entwined with that of religious sentiments. One poster in striking yellow, contains a poster of Rahul Gandhi, and its message is: *Bhartiya Dhwaj hi mera dharm hai* (Indian Flag is my religion). This is an effort to bring in the nationalist discourse to the people, and to tell them that we are all part of the same ethos. It may be read as an effort to intervene in a situation where the discontent against the state (which is generally seen as a synonym for the nation) is quite acute. The elite is able to bind the votes through this discourse and one finds the Congress having a significant space here. The discourse of terrorism based on profiling of individuals of a particular religion, one which

also fosters a particular kind of right wing agenda on nationalism is very obvious in these posters. Fostering discourses of nationalism has been helpful to the ruling elite in subverting resistance and alternatives. All other feelings, sentiments, discontents get subsumed within the meta-narrative of nationalism. This creates an allegiance to Nation and when this particular idea of Nation is invariably synonymous with the capital it would mean to be allegiance to capital in the ultimate analysis. This is what happens beneath all these discourses. The working class remains at the margins, still groping for modes of mobilisation and retaliation that could bring its discourse to the forefront within the ghetto.

Two recent posters from the Congress use its old 'Hindu Muslim *bhai bhai*' (Hindus and Muslims are brothers) formula. The posters with leaders presented as icons, carries slogans like *Congress ke char sipahi, Hindu Muslim, Sikh, Isai* (Congress has four soldiers — Hindu, Muslim, Sikh and Christian). It also depicts anti-terrorist slogans like — *Shakil*

Saifi ne thana hai, Aatankwad mitana hai [Shakil Saifi (a local emerging politician) has pledged to weed out terrorism]. It still wants to convey the message that say that we are secular, can fight terrorism (the universal lingo of nationalist frenzy that allows hassle-free rule of capital) but at the same time have an all inclusive (religion wise) social base. But this idea doesn't have much value in the area. The last election saw a paradigmatic change when the Muslim brotherhood stood against the Congress after the Batla House incident. "People don't believe in Congress.... we don't trust any such party. .... *Hindustan mein aisi politics nahi hoti... yahan har community ko aage aa kar apna social base banana padta hai, jaise ki Mayawati ne kiya. Ek baar hum apna social base bana lein, phir dusri communities aur social justice ki baat kareinge*" ('Such politics does not happen in India... here every community has to come up and prepare their own social base like Mayawati did. Let us prepare our first and then we will talk about social justice and other communities') said SQR Iliyas, convener, AIMPLB (All India Muslim Personal Law Board) and Secretary, Jamat-e-Islami Hind about the political party Jamat-e-Islami was contemplating to launch.[10] People believe that the Congress won the elections because of the anti-incumbency factor. "How can we [Muslims] win the election, when we ourselves are divided", said Shakil Ahmed, a local resident, about the stupidity of fielding two Muslim candidates against Congress. Asif Khan, another resident, believes that the Congress won because of the Hindu votes from Khader and other surrounding areas. Congress posters in the Muslim area carry 'well wishes' on some Hindu festivals.

Interestingly, posters around the Shia mosque don't carry any political messages. They are mostly about religious practices, rituals, pilgrimages or about social upliftment. These posters reflect on the exclusivity of Shia doctrines and

10. See Appendix for a detailed interview

are only in Shia dominated areas, perhaps with the aim of addressing that specific constituency. On the other hand, posters of other religious organizations try to sound universalistic in by addressing the general concerns of the whole 'muslim' area including the Shia one. This effort to create a kind of universalism is evident in some of the posters dealing with community issues where Shia names also figure as signatories.

In most of its posters, the dominant political formation of the area, which has been winning the Assembly elections, the Congress, does not raise issues specific to the backwardness of the area. The plight of the poor, which is multidimensional, is also not raised in the posters, neither are demands for improving the infrastructural status of the area, reflected in bad roads, irregular water supply, horrible sanitation and drainage system, etc. The entire area has only one public toilet on the street heading towards Noornagar. It doesn't have any corporation dustbin and corporation water is not supplied to most of the area. Furthermore the drainage system is blocked at many places and the sever system is almost out of use with most people making their own safety tanks. But these issues are not highlighted in any of the posters. The living condition of the poor as well as the so-called middle class is pathetic. Most of the poor say that they have not been issued BPL (Below Poverty Line) cards. Employment opportunities are few and help from the state is scarce. However, posters have only been trying to appeal to people on issues of discrimination (without any specificity), reservation, terrorism and so on.

One organisation has raised very distinct political issue - Ramdas Athawle's Republican Party of India. It raises the issue of water, construction and of labourers. It criticises the existing leadership for being incompetent. It is the only party which talks about the labourers. But it also talks about lifting ban on construction in the area.

Curiously it doesn't talk about issues of lower caste Muslims which should be an obvious issue for a Dalit party. It confirms to the dominant monolithic identity of Muslims. Yet it doesn't have any prominent Muslim leaders on its posters. The posters are in Hindi and have pictures of Ambedkar, Athawale and that of the local party leaders. It can be read as an effort to expand its base in the areas where nearly all political organisations are present.

The posters put up by the different organisations show how the crafting of a collective Muslim identity takes place *internally*, based on opportunities created by *external* factors. The organisations organise themselves and the whole community in accordance with a particular programmatic agenda. The idea of a collective identity, which obfuscates the internal class conflicts within the community, emerges from these symbols. Such symbols become vital sources of strengthening the constitution of such an identity.

Spaces in our society get organised and reorganised according to the historical necessities of the area. *In the process of organisation and reorganisation, the diverse symbols of everyday life, created by the organisations as embodiments of the local situations and represented in the different imageries, strengthen the sense of a collective identity, underplaying the class dynamics that exists within as the driving force of everyday social relations.* One simple example of the reorganisation of the city is the pushing out of slum dwellers from the core of the city during the neoliberal regime in India. The other example can be found in the way cities in Gujarat have reorganised themselves along religious grounds (Breman, 2002). When such an organisation or reorganisation happens the role of external factors becomes very significant, and one external factor appears to be that of governmentality. This is the element that connects the people to the state in their everyday lives and includes the different instruments of the state that are supposed to be in constant connection with the masses. It is altogether a different issue (which will not be considered here) whether that connection in the everyday lives of people becomes a means of surveillance or not. The situation in and around the area where the fieldwork was carried out has a history of conflicts with the coercive machineries of state (see Gramsci (2004) regarding the idea of coercion and consent), like the police force. Generally these aspects of identity formation are missed out as the celebration of multiple subjectivities occupies centrestage in name of the democratisation process, the diffusion of justice and of egalitarian principles providing the metanarrative of capital an escape route. In documentations riots in the recent past have been found to be planned well in advance, with evidence of participation of the state (Breman, 1993, p. 738) and of its "administrative connivance" (Gupta, 2002). It is important to mention this because once the complicity of the state becomes evident, the concept of a citizenship that bases itself in a certain democratic framework founded on the principle of equality, becomes questionable. It facilitates the process of a collective identity formation and the 'other' begins defining itself anew in the light of the new politico-economic situation. This process which constructs the idea of the 'other' is not (1) a spontaneous, momentary event; (2) neither is it a purely cultural phenomenon; and (3) nor is it a purely religion based or personalised phenomenon. In fact, this construction has a historical baggage and is intrinsically related to the political economy as in the case of the emergence of right wing assertions world over.

For instance, in September 2007, the residents attacked the police station/post in Jamia Nagar and Shaheen Bagh and clashed with police personnel when a policeman, allegedly, desecrated (threw it down along with other things from a make shift shop in the busy market place) their holy book – the Quran – in the market place. The violence which happens in the area emerges out of the context that is central to the area. This is a context which combines the general frustration of the local masses and directs it against the instruments of state.[11] The process of identity formation which gets an impetus through these incidents that allow their self-portrayal as well portrayal by 'outsiders' as the

11. It is relevant to reiterate that a particular image of the whole area in the vicissitudes of Jamia Millia Islamia, which is predominantly inhabited by Muslim population, has been constructed – as a site which harbours terrorists. This image has been vindicated by the way repressive state machineries swoop down on the whole area after any 'act of terror'. Before the September 2008 encounter about which different sections of society have articulated their reservations, a similar situation had arisen in December 2000 after the Red Fort attack. (see http://www.indianexpress.com/ie/daily/20001228/ina28057.html). There have been other instances as well when local residents foiled attempts to kidnap young men by the NOIDA police (see http://www.twocircles.net/2008oct16/jamia_residents_foiled_encounter_attempt.html)

'other'.[12] This pattern of identity formation is also consolidated by the local elite, which prefers a certain kind of state non-interference so as to continue illegal constructions, land transactions and other economic activities such as small time industrial units that flout labour laws and where surplus maximisation happens through extra-coercive means of labour exploitation. In such circumstances the politics of collective identity allows this elite to secure its interests. Hence, the collective identity gets created as part of the *externality* as well as the *internality* of production relations. And it is important to mention that the production relations are in a certain sense localised (within the collective) but not autonomous, they exist in dynamic, dialectical relationship with the metanarrative of capital.

It is from this dynamics of *internality* and *externality* that emerges the issue of how in situations of heightened conflict with the 'other' community it is the cleavage of class that exposes itself. Chakravarti in his work highlights that

> "(i) the principal victims of the violence and ghettoisation are by and large poor Muslims in rural and urban areas. They exist today outside the margins of mainstream Indian society in two very fundamental senses: firstly, in terms of material well-being, and secondly, as citizens; (ii) the alienation of poor Muslims is attributable to the process of saffronisation which diverts attention from the sources of poverty and oppression in Gujarat society. The real

12. The idea of the 'other' is based in a certain kind of nationalist discourse that makes Muslims anti-national, always wanting them to prove their credentials as nationalists has been debated by a lot of people. In fact, it is argued that they have been systematically discriminated against even by the state, which claims to represent a secular ethos, by not including them in government jobs or in decision-making positions, which claims to represent a secular ethos (GOI, 2006; Hasan, 2009).

> oppressors of the underclass at large therefore continue to prosper" (2002, p. 4246).

He furthers his argument by saying that in a situation such as the one in Gujarat, the process of saffronisation and its politics of hate demonstrated in unrelenting street violence provides the hitherto marginalised 'powerless' Dalits and *adivasis* a sense of power which results in "the possibilities of unrestrained looting of the properties of Muslims". In a situation where Hindutva becomes the dominant ideology, it is not surprising

> "that sections belonging to such groups have been inspired by an enormous perverse zeal to kill, hack and burn Muslims, in spite of the fact that the latter might be as oppressed as they are.
>
> In such circumstances the poor Muslim indeed stands totally abandoned by the rest of society. In every respect that the community as a whole has been victimised, the trauma for those who are poor is manifold. The intensity of the ghettoisation suffered by the Muslims in general is formidable, but it is even worse for those whose meagre possessions have been destroyed. Even their labour power, the pre-eminent means of keeping body and soul together, carries little value in a social setting where the community is subjected to the economic boycott called by the Vishwa Hindu Parishad (VHP), a key constituent of the *Sangh parivar* (Chakravarti, 2002, p. 4248).

Hence, what becomes amply clear is that the Muslim community cannot be taken as a homogeneous entity because of its sharp class based polarisation, which makes the poor Muslim suffer more when the onslaught of the 'other' takes place. The class politics within the community *is* significant, but is never *given* that significance. Rather, the Muslim question which has acquired tremendous political significance, as evident from the effort of different political formations to bring them to their side, indicates attempts at evolving an understanding of the community as homogeneous and undifferentiated. There have been studies, which point towards the heterogeneity of the community in caste terms (Ahmad, 1973; Bhatty, 1996; Anwar, 2001) as well as along class lines. It had been argued by Habib et.al. (1976, p. 68) that while

> "Muslim masses are exceptionally hard pressed, the Muslims are not a totally 'depressed' community. There are large numbers of Muslim landlords and semi-capitalistic farmers (beneficiaries of the Green Revolution), merchants and upto-medium-scale industrialists, who dominate the Muslim community politically as the bulwark of reactionary forces within it, and often serve as agents of the Congress and other bourgeois-landlord parties".

However, the political rhetoric of the Muslim elite as well as of communal politics tends to underplay these distinctions. One very recent and ongoing debate regarding reservations reflects the segmentation of the community along class and caste lines and the predominance of the 'upper caste' elite view on the issue, which argues for reservation for the religious community as a whole. A complete denial of the inherent fracturing of the community is responsible for the absence of reservation for Backward Castes and Dalits within Muslims. This has been interpreted by some as an effort to maintain the hegemony of the 'upper caste' elite section within the religious community. The example of non-implementation of OBC reservation as decided by the Supreme Court of India within the Jamia Millia Islamia is may be considered an effort by entrenched interests within the community to retain their control over institutions such as this.[13] Interestingly, such denial of

13. This emerged during one of the group discussions in the field, which was attended by some young researchers and students.

reservations happens, with tacit support of the state because it allows the institution to prolong its non-implementation, when 40.7 per cent of the Muslim population is categorised as OBC, and their share among the OBC population of the country is around 15.7 per cent (Hasan, 2009).

However, what has been described above in the context of the area near the Jamia Millia Islamia does not only have a clear cut definition in terms of physical location (separate as it is from the other part of the city) but also allows it to develop its own sense of community and a certain kind of economy (that obviously does work by egalitarian principles). It is in this context that one may characterise the area as a *ghetto* (which will be discussed subsequently).

Chapter 4

Identity Politics and Ghettoisation[14]

The segregation of our society on various grounds is universally recognised and a great deal of literature also points towards stark and ever increasing polarisation on basis of class. Social science in India has been divided over the primary nature of stratification of Indian society – some arguing for caste and others for class. And gender is seen as impinging upon all categories as creating a division between men and women. If one looks at a city, and to my mind Delhi figures as an immediate example, one finds another significant kind of segregation – physical segregation along religious lines. There are areas in the city where a particular religious community dominates, such as Jamia Nagar and its adjoining areas. The identification of this area as belonging to a particular religious community is such that in recent months it has been pointed out that people residing there find it difficult to even access basic amenities. The formation of the city space has been such that one gets today starkly divided habitations based on different religious identities, specifically Muslim and non-Muslim. One could see how the majoritarian mental structure does not provide any space to

---

14. Ghetto is understood, here, as a physical space within the city which gets constituted historically as a symbol of socio-cultural isolation of a particular community vis-à-vis the majority/other communities.

Muslims in their imagination when cases of Muslims being denied houses on rent appeared in the media. This is not to suggest that the formation of ghettos can be traced only to the increasing religious polarisation in the city. But this study bases itself on the fact that there is a stark presence of zones of Hindus and Muslims in the city. And through fieldwork it would try to explore the diversity of factors that results in ghetto formation as well as the political economy of such ghettos.

There is more to the phenomenon of ghetto formation than it appears. It hides within itself the dynamics and politics of a collective identity formation. It is a site where different identities interact with each other. This interaction reveals the reasons for formation of collective identities, as well as the way in which such formations are sustained. Some argue that the identities get constituted through the principle of competition – a competition which is rooted in the question of survival – the working class of one religious community competing with that of another for survival or the elite of one religious community competing with that of another. This competition is different for the two segments mentioned above – while the competition of the elite allows expansion of capital and therefore progress of capitalism and its agents, the competition among the working class weakens them and does not allow them to resist the rule of capital, or even understand how capital furthers its rule through identities and different symbolisms. There are others who question this analysis of collective identity formation raising the question as to how would one explain the emergence of religion based ghettos, where the defining features of the collective are religious and are constituted out of insecurity of one religious community vis-à-vis the other as well as out of the politics of majoritarianism.

In such cases one encounters certain obvious questions – how does the economy of the ghetto work?; is it a self-sufficient economy?; in the production process that sustains the economic life (as well as the social life) of the ghetto where are the different class constituents of the heterogeneous community located?; how do they interact with each other?; is the religious basis overriding their economic or social hierarchisation thereby bringing in an equalising effect? Such questions need a deeper probe into the very functionality of the ghetto (its economics and politics). This would explain the internal dynamics of the ghetto which needs to be seen as in a constant dialectical relation with the outside world. It is only through this dialectics that one would understand how ghetto formation at one level, allows a better control by the core (or the classes or socio-religious communities in power or owing allegiance to the class or socio-religious community in power) of the everyday political and economic affairs of others (the classes or socio-religious communities on the margins of economy and society). The mechanical division of the city allows easier manipulation of policies (a point that has been mentioned even by empirical reports referred here)[15] and politics. At another level this division tries to construct a world which is autonomous, thereby limiting the political perspective of others vis-à-vis the politics of the core. In other words, the people staying within these areas become easier targets for manipulation by not only the dominant, ruling sections of the larger society but also by their own elite within the ghetto.

However, there have not been many studies on the phenomenon of ghettoisation in India except for the term being increasingly used to measure the impact of right wing fundamentalism in cities such as Ahmedabad. The assertion of right wing fundamentalism towards the closing decades of the 20th century and the beginning of the 21st century created a situation of insecurity and resulted in, what

15. See JMI, Action Aid and ISI (2006) for details

Álvarez-Rivadulla (2007) calls in a different context, creation of 'gated communities'. It is in this context that the present study on ghettos is proposed.

Such a study is important for reasons, which are academic as well as political. The studies of identities and identity formation, which have appeared in great numbers recently, make it important to examine the subject critically and with a perspective, which is generally not used while studying identity formation, namely the class perspective. Secondly with the developments which appear 'political' (for those who believe in value neutrality of the academia and further distinguish between politics and academics as mutually exclusive) resulted in far reaching consequences it has become important that one (1) breaks the notion of collective identities as homogeneous, (2) examines the class dimensions in the functionality of identities; and (3) contextualises identity politics and its processes in the political economy of the system.

Studies on ghettos emerged as a major area of research in societies characterised by divisions of the population on lines of race and colour. Hence, one comes across studies on ghettos based on colour in North America, those based on ethnicity and race in Latin America as well as some European countries. The word "ghetto" has been used in numerous contexts and has carried various meanings across a long historical timeline. The Oxford English Dictionary says that the term is probably Italian in origin and was perhaps used for the first time in Venice, around 1516, to describe a neighbourhood on the site of the city's foundry. "The first recorded written use of the word occurred in 1611 in Coryat's Crudities, in which he describes "the place where the whole fraternity of the *Iews* (sic) dwelleth together, which is called the Ghetto." After this initial use, the word appears infrequently in written form until the late 19th century, when the social landscape of the city becomes the subject of many authors and scholars (Pearson, 2003). The 20th century saw an extensive use of the term in social sciences and a burgeoning literature on the theme emerged. A great deal of sociological work on ghettos also started appearing in the country which experienced it a major way, i.e., the USA. In fact, the amount of material that has been produced on ghettos has been such that it led scholars to remark that "ghetto literature, the product of intense feeling and dramatic experience, has always been the most readable material of American urban history, indeed the only books which could command a wide audience" (Warner, Jr. and Burke, 1969).[16]

In the USA "the term 'ghetto' was first used to describe the immigrant quarters of American cities at the turn of the nineteenth century when large numbers of east European Jews settled in the congested inner sections of north-eastern and mid-western cities. Although in some north-eastern cities there had been small Sephardic communities since the

---

16. The authors go on to show that "both literary tradition and current interest create a severe historical distortion". This distortion appears in the way a picture of integration of American society through the diffusion of immigrants and their descendants" happened and later a "suburban intermixture" also developed. They argue that though assimilation happened but "assimilation by way of a ghetto has always been a limited case in American urban history, limited both in time span and in membership. Most foreign immigrants to American cities never lived in ghettos, and most immigrant ghettos that did exist were the product of the largest cities and the eastern and southern European immigrants of I880-I940. Moreover, if a ghetto be defined as a place inhabited almost exclusively by one ethnic group, then only the caste- isolated northern Negro has an extended tradition of ghetto living. Only the northern Negro has had a heavy preponderance of his group confined to a segregated quarter of a city" (Warner, Jr. and Burke, 1969, pp. 173-74).

colonial period and somewhat larger groups of German Jews since the middle of the nineteenth century, the term ghetto was rarely, if ever, used to describe their residential quarters" (Ward, 1982, p. 257). "Like the term 'slum', the ghetto was described as a place where there was a related combination of unhealthy living quarters, isolation from the remainder of urban society and pathological social conditions; but in the ghetto, the presence of exotic migrants compounded the problems of the slum" (ibid, pp. 258-259). The negative connotations attached with the term ghetto have also altered. Immigrants living in slums and creating pathological conditions is no longer the sense attributed to the ghettos in North America, argues Ward. Rather, "the term 'ghetto' may now be used to describe any highly clustered ethnic group irrespective of whether they are materially deprived, socially disorganized or concentrated in the inner city" (ibid, p. 257).

"The ghetto thus became a symbol of the social isolation of those immigrants who were unlikely to assimilate to American society" (ibid, p. 260). With changes in policies and reduction in immigration, the ghettos came to be seen as temporary quarters. It was largely believed that the people living in the Ghettos will be assimilated. Ward also critiques the misconceptions attached to the original meaning of 'ghetto' as a place where unhygienic conditions led to high mortality etc. He engages with the idea saw ghettos as constituted by people who lost their cultural roots as they got assimilated and argued that, rather, there were evidences of how people of different ethnic or racial group such as the Indians retained their culture while living in exclusivity. However, it has been proved beyond doubt after the Katrina, how certain cities, suburban areas and places of residence are not only ignored and neglected by the state because they are inhabited by people of a particular race but people are left to die on a mass scale due to such a neglect and the nation and the state remains 'normal'. McLaren and Jaramillo write that "coiled like a viper in the hurricane's eye, the Specter of Capitalism unleashed its pent-up supply of hell on its historically most vulnerable victims: impoverished African Americans" (McLaren and Jaramillo, 2007, p. 205). The post-Katrina Hurricane New Orleans' experience debunked the façade of an America that was no longer racist. Even if figures on prison inmates (majority are blacks and Hispanics) or the number of poor concentrated more among these people, were raising questions on the idea of a democracy free of racism that was supposed to have been born out of the Civil Rights Movement, Katrina reiterated that even segregation in terms of housing and physical concentration of poor and African Americans persisted.

> "It was an attack on hope: hope that the United States had overcome its historical legacy of racism, hope that educated journalists had moved beyond portraying life in the United States with brutally overt or subtle racist stereotypes, hope that capitalist democracies had made necessary headways in ending poverty, hope that the government could muster whatever it took to care for its poor and dispossessed in a time of emergency. Katrina sounded the death knell of such a hope, a hope born in the crucible of the Civil Rights Movement of earlier—and seemingly much more unreal—times" (McLaren and Jaramillo, 2007, p. 205).

Work on ghettos has been flourishing in the USA since the beginning of the 20th century. Louis Wirth came up with his work called *The Ghetto* in 1928. He laid out a theory of ghetto formation and looked at the processes that went into its making and then explored how they got gradually dismantled through a process of assimilation (Wirth, 1928). He argued that ghettos as an institution should be an area of interest for a sociologist "because it represents a prolonged case study in isolation. It may be regarded as a form of accommodation through which a minority has effectively been subordinated to a dominant group. The ghetto exhibits at least one historical form of dealing with a dissenting minority within a larger population, and as such has served as an instrument of control. At the same time the ghetto represents a form of toleration through which a *modus vivendi* is established between groups that are in conflict with each other on fundamental issues"(Wirth, pp. 57-58). His points of reference were the Jewish ghettos, but he argues that understanding them will prove beneficial to understand the modern ghettos as well as, they still serve some of those functions.

Ghettos in West largely represented "the actual processes of distribution and grouping of the population" and Wirth attributes characteristics to ghettos which make them appear in a positive light; they appear as a medium through which cultural groups express their "heritages"; it explains the dynamics of population "sifting and resifting" which assigns "locations to each section"; it becomes a mode of maintaining the integrity and continuity of a community; and it reflects the way a "cultural community is transformed by degrees until it blends with the larger community about it" (ibid, p. 58).

He argues that the "ancestry" of the modern ghetto can be traced back to the medieval European urban institutions. And he makes an effort to understand ghettos through the Jewish ghettos, arguing that they had emerged "informally" (ibid, p. 57), wherein the Jews lived as separate communities not due to any "external pressure or by deliberate design" but because of their tradition, habits, customs. In fact for the Jews their separation offered "the best opportunity for following their religious percepts, their established ritual and diet, and the numerous functions which tied the individual to familial and communal institutions" (ibid, p. 59). The locally separated communities also provided a kind of "freedom from hostile criticism and the backing of a group of kindred spirits" for the immigrants (ibid, p. 60). The ghetto provided an individual a sense of community, a support base and took care of alienation that he may suffer in the process of his interactions with the external world. But such an "instrumentality", Wirth argues, gradually distanced the Jew from the remainder of population. "These barriers did not completely inhibit contact, but they reduced it to the type of relationships which were of a secondary and formal nature" (ibid, p. 61), the external world being formal and the internal one being informal. Gradually with changes in history, the forms of community life that "had arisen naturally and spontaneously" became "formalised" as legal enactments. Wirth, however, arguing strongly against the idea of a ghetto as stagnant, held that the internal life of the ghetto was very vibrant. The solidarity of the ghetto was derived from the family life and religious symbols. The life within the ghetto was "well organised, and custom and ritual played an institutionalising role" (ibid, p. 63).

Wirth made an effort to reflect on ghetto life of contemporary USA and argued that wherever the interaction between the immigrants and the original settlers continued for long ghettoisation has disappeared. In fact, Wirth goes on to conclude that "what has happened in the case of Jews is essentially what has happened in all minority groups in recent times. As the barriers of isolation have receded, social intercourse and interbreeding have decimated the size of the group and levelled its distinguishing characteristics to those of the milieu" (ibid, p. 67).

The ideas and the understanding put forth by Wirth regarding ghettos has been critiqued in great detail (Etzioni, 1959; Baldwin, 2004). Wirth saw urban design and development as part of some natural process of growth rather than deliberate (Baldwin, 2004, p. 417), an idea which cleared up further with the emergence of the idea of the 'second ghetto' (Hirsch, 1998; Seligman, 2003; Mohl, 2003)) Etzioni argued that Wirth's work, *The Ghetto*, was inspired by Park's model of a natural history of race and ethnic relations and it sees the pattern of interaction among different ethnic groups as passing through "the stages of isolation, competition, conflict, and accommodation" ultimately resulting into assimilation of the minority group (Etzioni, 1959, p. 255). This is a scheme, which can be proved through contradictory data as well, as it builds an ambience of ambiguity and vacuum in social research. Etzioni questions the scientificity of the scheme itself and says that it does not allow any space for any alternative and offers only a fixed possibility of assimilation. For instance, "when an ethnic group is assimilating, it is suggested that the hypothesis is supported; if an ethnic group is not assimilating, it is suggested that it has not yet reached the stage of assimilation" (ibid, p. 255).

Wirth's ideas seem to paint a picture of the social dynamics as something which is quite simple, uncomplicated and undialectical. He does not see the diverse forces operating in a society and impinging upon each other effecting fundamental changes in social relations. Due to this lack, he sees assimilation as a natural process in society. Etzioni raises this question by pointing out that though the processes of assimilation are analyzed clearly in Wirth – marriage and conversion being the two mechanisms – he fails to elaborate on the "conditions under which the processes of assimilation are triggered or blocked" (ibid, 1959, p. 256). Because Wirth, along with Park, consider the process of assimilation as natural, they introduce "adhoc" factors as responsible for delays and blocks.

For Wirth the coming of Hitler would be an accident in history that led to the ghettoisation of Jews and eventually through the process which he describes the Jews get assimilated within the larger society. Because of the absence of a historical materialist understanding, Wirth could not locate the emergence of fascism/Nazism in the political economy of capitalism and therefore fails to explain why neo-nazi groups have resurfaced all across Europe towards the end of 20th century or why right-wing politics has emerged all over the globe. Fascism emerges at particular historical conjunctures due to specific historical reasons. Towards the closing decades of the 20th century fascist parties became "part of the established landscape in almost every country of Europe" (Renton, 2007, p. 08)[17] and even in other countries in different parts of the globe, for instance in India. And their emergence is merely through force or coercive take over of the state but they emerge as a part of the 'democratic process'. Similarly, one could observe the tendency of fascist parties becoming respectable, "so aspects of fascist thinking have been allowed to enter into the realm of polite intellectual debate" (ibid, p. 11). Hence, one finds that fascism resurfaces time and again in history. Renton argues that

> "...fascism is a recurrent response to the conditions under capitalism. Because capitalism goes into crisis, because it forces millions into unemployment, so there are conditions in which bitterness grows. Because capitalism itself relies on a series of ideas, and because these include racism and elitism, so capitalism constantly fills the reservoir of reactionary ideas that fascism relies on to grow (ibid, p. 115).

A social scientist working on lines of Wirth remains in no position to understand the processes which go into making of historical products. It is this lack due to which Wirth and others following similarly fallacious methodological orientations, fail to look at the issue of ghettoisation as evolving out of historical processes which emerge out of concrete historical conditions. An obvious consequence of such an understanding would be to consider moments as *given*, as *particularities* which are *autonomous*. Thus, the

17. Also see Renton, Dave (2001) *This Rough Game: Fascism and Anti-fascism*, Sutton Publishing, Gloucester

emergence of fascism would not seem to have anything to do with the crisis of capitalism or with the need of the bourgeoisie to entrench itself firmly in power, to avert any possibility of the defeat of capitalism. Formation of ghettos, along similar lines, are not merely representations of a deep rooted polarisation that occurs within the system, which *excludes* certain sections or *compels* them to huddle together due to insecurity from the 'other'. Ghettos formed along purely economic lines may be due to a particular stage of capitalist development, as is happening in Indian cities in the neoliberal phase. In other words, *moments* or *particularities* need to be seen as embedded in the system, emerging out of the inherent character of the system.

However, Wirth fails to take cognizance of this functional aspects of the system and also fails to locate ghettos within this framework. His argument fails to look at the issue of alternatives for the 'other' communities, a point which Etzioni suggests (but not from within the Marxian framework), when he says that groups come into contact with each other "by the process of technological, economic, and social change, and perhaps this is an unavoidable process, the remaining stages should be seen as *alternative situations* rather than links in an evolutionary process culminating in assimilation. Groups are either in conflict or accommodation or assimilation. It is the task of social science to inquire into the conditions under which this or that alternative is chosen" (Etzioni, 1959, p. 256). Etzioni goes on to argue that Wirth, following Park, "maintains that the Ghetto, and with it the Jews, are bound to assimilate and to disappear sooner or later as a distinct group" (ibid, p. 256). This may, if extended further indicate an undemocratic conception of social, political and economic life. A linear pattern of life and an argument for the sustenance of the *status quo*, or the dominant paradigm, is being reinforced by Wirth.

A historicised understanding of the processes of social

formation that emerges out of a certain conjuncture of production process/relations, therefore, becomes an essential tool for understanding the society in general and the process of ghetto formation in particular. It will be relevant to recall Marx here, who wrote in his *Preface to A Contribution to the Critique of Political Economy*:

> "In the social production of their existence, men inevitably enter into definite relations, which are independent of their will, namely relations of production appropriate to a given stage in the development of their material forces of production. The totality of these relations of production constitutes the economic structure of society, the real foundation, on which arises a legal and political superstructure and to which correspond definite forms of social consciousness. The mode of production of material life conditions the general process of social, political and intellectual life. It is not the consciousness of men that determines their existence, but their social existence that determines their consciousness" (Marx, 1977, p. 503).

Collective identity is the defining feature of ghettos. Therefore, one cannot really separate the political economy of identity formation from that of a ghetto. Historically, in the city of Delhi there have been areas which could be identified along religious lines. Old Delhi, while it housed different communities at one point of time, got reduced to being primarily a Muslim area. Similar are the cases of Nizamuddin and some colonies in East Delhi. The idea of habitat itself comes to be defined along religious lines. While it is true that religious polarisation was seen as early as the pre-independence days, the memories of the past also become important determinants of closed-ness of communities. The politics of right wing assertion in Independent India, which became rampant in the closing decades of the 20th century furthered the idea of communities living together in one place. *In this work, a ghetto has been understood as a segregated physical location which is used by a community (cutting across regions and classes) as a site of habitation. This segregation is to maintain a distinct cultural ethos, to remain safely in a huddled space where the majoritarian 'other' does not intervene and dictate everyday affairs and to be free to exercise their own religion.* However, such a location raises several questions: can such a site be possible today when there are discourses like that of globalisation trying to bring people together?; can there be a common will of people cutting across class lines to stay at one place out of certain politico-religious compulsions?; is it only the external factors or are there internal factors as well which are responsible for formation of such sites, which are called ghettos here?

Studies of ghettoisation comprise a relatively marginal field in the Indian social sciences. Breman talks of two rounds of ghettoisation. In the first round people belonging to the same community start living in blocks dominated by their own community and in cases of tension the peacemakers from the community would act as negotiators to keep any possibility of a violent rift at bay. In the second round of ghettoisation, this could no longer remain possible as the members of the minority are driven out of localities (2002, p. 1486). This process happened because the institutions that provided spaces and opportunities for dialogue disappeared from the face of our public life (Suhurd, 2002). "The trend towards spatial segregation which already began several decades ago should be understood as both cause and effect of the erosion of intercommunal networks" (Breman, 2002, p. 1486). All forms of institutions and forums that would inculcate principles of dissent and resistance (which are essential features of the democratisation process) have been weakened and, therefore, the unemployed, informalised labour force that lives a precarious existence has no modes of expressing its discontent and anger, that is easily used by the ruling class in forms of their involvement in communal violence. It also, quite significantly, allows the discontent against the system to be weakened. This is a what happens not only in the case of Hindu but also Islamic fundamentalism.

Apart from the study by Breman in the context of Gujarat, efforts have been made by some other studies to understand the process as well. One study argues that Muslims are victims of "forced ghettoisation"; after the communal riots and pogroms they have been compelled to shift to Muslim dominated areas in search of a sense of security. "Many middle class Muslims too, prefer living in such areas although the levels of infrastructural provision are poor and even though they can afford living in more 'posh', 'upper' class Hindu-dominated areas" (JMI, et al., 2006, p. 109). Apart from affecting the economic and educational condition of inhabitants the ghettos reduce possibilities of inter-community interaction and leads "to the strengthening of an insular mentality, because of which the community is not able to properly articulate its views and concerns before a wider public. It also strengthens the hold of conservative religious forces" (ibid, p. 109). The empirically grounded studies in localities of Delhi and Gujarat point out how the migration towards Muslim majority areas even at the cost of economic opportunities is high due to a feeling of insecurity.

Hence, apart from looking at how ghettos are formed, it is essential to look at the historical processes that give birth to such formations. The arguments presented above point out how religious ghettos may get formed through a constant political process of positing one community against another (it is important to mention that there are intrinsic problems with even categorising everyone as belonging to one community at an equal plane, because it homogenises them and constructs a basis for identity politics, that furthers the goals of the elite within the community). It may also be understood as a process whereby the elite within Muslims carved out a physical, and therefore a political, space for its own interests. Through this process a world is constructed, of institutions, common people and gradually a small economic and political space is carved out which furthers the consolidation of a collective identity. The areas where we conducted our fieldwork are not exceptions to this process. A recent research on Zakir Nagar points out how it is explicitly becoming a Muslim neighbourhood. "Residents described how as Hindus moved out of the neighbourhood and new Muslim migrants moved in, the area changed from being a teachers' colony to being a markedly Muslim colony, thus replacing professional with religious identity" (Kirmani, 2007, p. 131).

Chapter 5

Why Study the Ghettos: Some Methodological Considerations

Scholars would argue that the world around us is defined across various levels – ranging from class, gender, caste, religion based divisions to those based on different kinds of cultural characteristics. However, there are always certain pitfalls in recognising these levels, and these pitfalls arise from certain methodological lacunae in our understanding. One problem emerges when we tend to look at the world as fragmented and celebrate particulars as expressions of democracy. Hence, discourses across many theoretical endeavours have focussed on the significance of the *local* over *global*. The idea of a universal has come under scathing criticism, especially from the postmodernists. Inbuilt into the postmodern scheme of thought has been the denunciation of the universal – "... its total acceptance of the ephemerality, fragmentation, discontinuity, and the chaotic..." (Harvey, 2000, p. 44). Al-Azmeh (2003) goes on to critique post-modernism for giving primacy to recognition and for being anti-historical. He writes that

> "The late capitalist, postmodern emphasis on self-referentiality and self-representation, the drift towards conceiving difference as incommensurability, the cognitive nihilism associated with postmodernism, the dissolution of objects of ethnographic study into 'voices' – all this, to my minds, leads to rejecting the tools of the historical and social

> sciences implicitly, even if in most cases inadvertently and unreflectively, in favour of an irrationalist and anti-historicist sympathetic sociology of singularity, and of an instinctivist theory of culture which tends, with its vitalist metaphysics, to collapse knowledge into being by relating it not to cognition, but to recognition, and particularly recognition of the collective self" (2003, p. 38).

The critique of class as the dominant form of social relation and Marxism as a theoretical endeavour emanated from the discourses which looked at Marxism as representing a universal. The argument being made here is not about putting up a defence of a particular school of thought but the effort is to raise a larger methodological question regarding the relationship among *particulars* and between *particular* and *universal*.

The issue, which is a methodological one, is that of understanding the ghettos as *particulars* as well as *universals*. In other words, a ghetto may be characterised by its own class and caste dynamics and therefore, there is a need to look at the interplay of this class dynamics in everyday life as well as in moments of crisis such as communal violence, state aggression, in the process of profiling or in terms of their political allegiance. In this sense, ghettos become universal units comprising of particulars such as regional politics or politics of caste and class as its internal attributes. But in today's situation where the rule of capital has penetrated every sphere of our existence, the ghettos also become particulars in themselves when it comes to their interaction with the world outside. This interaction reveals the bearing of the larger system towards the ghetto – for instance how does the larger system through its policies and politics looks at the resettled slums or how does the majoritarian Hindu society and polity looks at the Muslim ghettos. However, we need to unravel this further to understand this dialectics of particular and universal: such as how do different segments within the ghetto interact with the world outside – with the ruling class politics as well as the politics of the dominated. One may find differences in perspective and actions between segments of the population. For instance, who suffers when profiling of one community happens? Whose livelihood is threatened? How does the economy of different kinds of ghettos work? Despite suffering, the poor may still go along the elite when the latter bargains with the elite outside. Apart from the fact that it is a natural consequence of identity politics, one needs to interrogate whether such an alliance remains the only viable option of survival for the oppressed of the ghettoised communities.

But before one explores these questions it becomes essential to understand how one would go about unravelling them. One way of looking at the question is in the immediacy of incidents and events that unfold, which may provide us with insights into the way a particular community is looked at but such an approach may not reveal to us the profundity of such situations because we do not look at how different classes within the religious community respond to it or participate in it. But, there may be another approach to understanding the situation or the 'Muslim Question' by asking questions such as: is this question the same for every Muslim? Are there Muslims who are affected by such situations more or less than others? What kind of distinctions exists within the Muslim community emerging out of the production process? Are problems of inaccessibility, deprivation and wretchedness shown by the Sachar Commission same for every Muslim? Or is it reflective of a sharp vertical polarisation in Muslim society, an accumulation of benefits by a very small minority leaving the vast mass impoverished?

A great amount of data is available which indicates that the dismal economic and educational status of Muslims in the country (GOI, 2006; NSSO, 2001). However, this data tells us the story of Muslims vis-à-vis the other communities (and their condition is definitely deplorable on that account). There are hardly any studies that would narrate the economic differentiation within the Muslim community. This becomes a methodological issue, and a contentious one, because firstly it determines the nature of the discourse on Muslims in the country, which is generally vis-à-vis an 'other' religious community; secondly, it constructs collective identity as the dominant political paradigm of such a large group of people who comprise the second largest religious group in the country[18]; thirdly, it rejects any possibility of conflict within the community along class lines and denies class as the determining principle of the politics that the elite of the community engages in.

While the Muslim question is a well debated issue (Sonalkar, 1993), there have been very few attempts that would look at how dynamics within the community work. It has been recognised that there is an elite within the community but how does it function vis-à-vis the larger systemic scenario is not well debated. The issue of everyday survival, in an increasingly polarised neoliberal world, and the pauperisation of the masses have failed to become political issues. The demand for jobs, land reforms, better amenities or even reservation on basis of caste has not been agenda for the Muslim leaders. Reasons have been quite obvious, but seldom acknowledged – the leadership is drawn from the elite or caters to the interests of the entrenched ruling caste and class of the Muslim community.

18. "The 2001 census enumerated India's Muslim population at over 138 million, and by 2006 the Muslim population would be over 150 million" (GOI, 2006).

Chapter 6

Identity Formation and the Ghetto: Reflections from the Field

An effort has been made in the earlier section to understand the historico-material processes that lead to the identity formation and also contributes towards formation of ghettos. In this section, the above mentioned framework is being used to understand how different aspects of identity formation interact in a field situation. Undertaken within a short span of time, the study restricted itself to a small number of respondents trying to provide the variety that would explain the attitude and understanding of different section of the Muslim society. Hence, four different categories were approached during the course of study. *Category A* included students who were students, studying in Jamia or any other institution and who reside in the area for education. They may be permanent residents of the area or they have migrated from other states to pursue their education, and would possibly search for jobs later in the same city. *Category B* included persons who own at least one house or a flat in the area. Occupationally, they either have their own business or a white collar job in the corporate sector, or stay here with their family. These respondents came here at least 10 years back. *Category C* included labourers, rickshaw pullers or petty shopkeepers such as tea stall owners, etc., (those owning grocery shops have been excluded from this category). Some of them stay in rented spaces, while some of them live with their families, and some others stay alone. Their wives and children live in their hometowns. Excluding rickshaw pullers all are planning to settle here. One of the labourers, who was our respondent, has already settled here with his family and stays in a rented accommodation. He married his daughter off to another labourer, who is also settled here. They stay in small, usually cramped houses and earn anything between Rs. 500 to 5000. *Category D* included people working in the organized corporate sector outside the area. They work in BPO's or have other middle level jobs and earn anything between Rs. 7000 to 40000 a month. Some of them come from lower middle class families but all aspire to get good jobs, accumulate wealth for an affluent lifestyle. Some of them live alone, while their families live back home, but all aspire to settle in Delhi as soon as possible with their families.

Table 1: Total Number of Respondents

	Bihar	*UP*	*Old Delhi*	*Any Other*	*Total*
A	12	1	2	0	15
B	7	3	3	2	15
C	9	0	4	4	17
D	9	4	6	0	19
Total	37	8	15	6	66

Source: Field Data

Of the total number of respondents the majority came from Bihar (See Chart No. 1). However, the sample also had people who migrated from Old Delhi and Uttar Pradesh. Migration had different meanings for different people ranging from purely economic to cultural and religious reasons.

Chart No.1

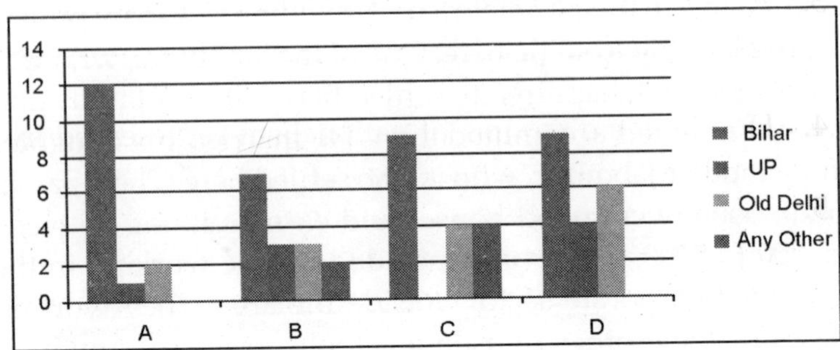

Source: Field Data

The qualitative data collected in the course of research included posters, their analysis, informal discussions as well as detailed informal and formal interviews. Interaction with people had become difficult due to a suspicion that people in the area have developed towards anything that appears to threaten them physically. This was more evident after the Batla house episode. In fact, at many places the researchers were questioned by people while they were photographing posters, or before answering their questions people asked them their religion. Due to the nature of events that unfolded and the kind of repression that had been unleashed by the police, media and the state as a whole it had become obvious why people developed this distrust towards individuals; this raises the pertinent issue of governmentality as well. It is based on these sources of data that an effort is made here to understand some questions:

1. How does an identity consolidate itself (for instance in moments of crisis such as the recent events)? What leads to the unity of diverse classes/castes in this process of consolidation?
2. Explore the role of cultural symbols and religious factors in constitution and sustenance of ghettos. Analyse how different segments interact with such

symbol and factor.

3. Analyse the symbols and representations in the public sphere which facilitate and foster the sense of collective identity.
4. How is the discourse of nationalism represented in the area and how do people look at it?
5. How does the elite of the community develop a discourse of collective identity? What are its frames of reference? Is it positing one religious community against the other? How is it manifested?
6. How is the caste and class differentiation within the Muslim society represented in this discourse and politics? What kind of political rhetoric is used to suppress such manifestations? How does the universal identity of a Muslim get constituted? In this process how are interests of the marginalised castes and classes suppressed?
7. How do different classes see their location vis-à-vis other classes within the ghetto as well as outside? How is the distinction represented in their everyday discourses, activities and politics? Are their pangs of a much needed horizontal class solidarity across religious groups? If no, why?
8. Is there any feeling among locals for a ghettoised existence? How do they view the issue?

Chart No. 2

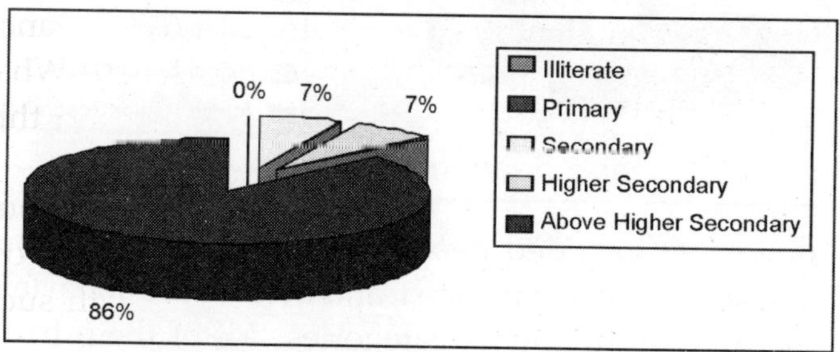

The educational background of Category A shows (Chart No. 2) that most of the respondents have qualifications above higher secondary. The educational levels are higher also because the respondents were primarily students.

On the other hand Category B of respondents (Chart No. 3), which included persons who either have their own business or have white collar jobs in the corporate sector, one finds the educational level higher, with number of illiterates being negligible.

Chart No. 3

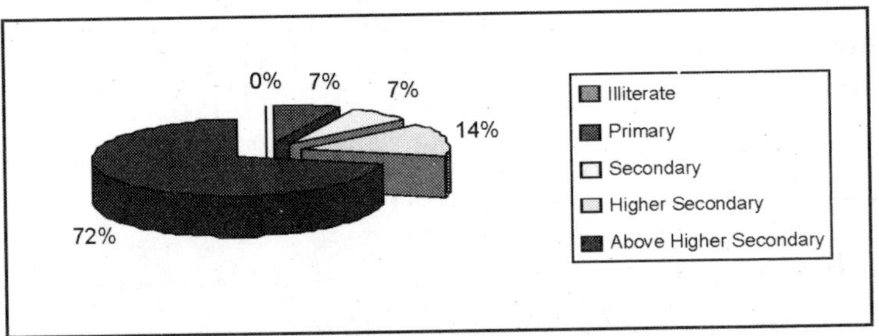

Category C (Chart No.4), which included primarily labourers, rickshaw pullers and petty shopkeepers, had lower educational levels compared to the earlier categories.

Chart No. 4

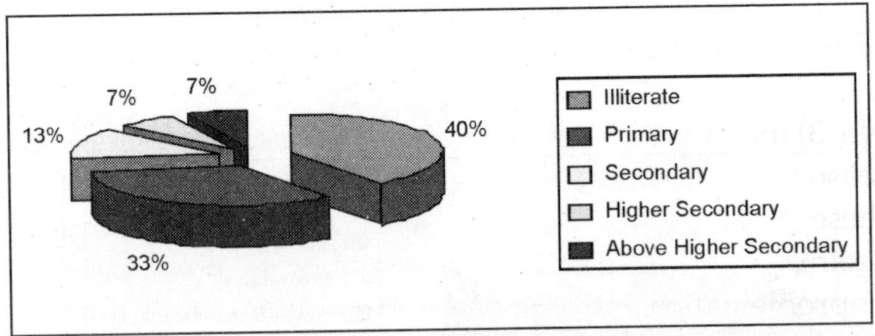

Category D included people working in the organised corporate sector outside the area, and their educational levels were the highest among all categories. All of them had an educational level beyond the higher secondary level.

The religious orientation of respondents was amply clear. The category of people who visit the *mazar* less are also those who consider *barelviat* as a result of ignorance. *Barelviat* as a stream of thought within Islam is believed to be more liberal and has been under constant attack from puritans. When the respondents were asked whether they would prefer to live in a Muslim neighbourhood majority responded in affirmative. Interestingly, the Category D, which comprises of people working in corporate sector quite a few preferred to stay in the area, which may be attributed to a kind of transition taking place due to integration into the market and into the aspirations and images generated by it (Table 2).

Table No. 2

	Preference for being in Muslim neighbourhood	*Visit mazar*	*Do your parents visit mazar*	*Part of jamaat*	*Is jamaat concerned about jamaat*	*Is barelviat due to ignorence*
A	8	3	4	4	4	11
B	8	4	6	6	7	13
C	13	10	10	4	7	4
D	5	3	4	6	9	12

Source: Field data

The table below indicates the extent to which the sense of collective identity is entrenched among the people who live in the area. The responses of categories A and D (Table No. 3) indicate that they do not see riots as a conspiracy. The reason may lie in the nature of knowledge formation that these two categories entail – they have formal educational 'training' which hammers constantly on us how State is an unproblematice entity and riot is more an act of deviance than as rooted in the politico-economic dynamics of the system. It also tells us about the how pedagogical practices become important sources of creating consensus in favour of the state and its hegemonic ideology. Over all responses to questions posed to them (evident in the table below) show their desire to have a stronger collective identity and the necessity to be united in order to overcome their problems.

Table No. 3

	Riots a conspiracy to finish off Muslims?	*Is Shahrukh Khan a Muslim?*	*Internal Divisions reason behind Muslim problem?*	*Muslims are victims of communalization b'coz they are not united?*
A	2	9	13	11
B	1	10	13	11
C	11	13	12	14
D	2	8	12	13

Source: Field data

While the feeling of the 'other' arising out of internal factors is amply clear from the above table there is a sense of the 'other' also generated in the everyday interactions with the outside world. This outside world was generally the workplace of people to whom we were talking to (see Table No.4). People working for non-Muslim employers or in a place which can be termed as a general/professional place of employment found it difficult to practice what they would prefer to, as follower of Islam, for instance the opportunity to pray was a problem. The respondents were quite aware of their Muslim identity at the workplace. In fact, if one tries to observe how a professional workplace functions one finds that any act which is different from the regular (which is essential for non-Muslim) such as *namaz* five times a day will be taken as odd. The other dimension of this problem is that irrespective of religion the professional ethics of capital dilutes practices which are time taking, because more time is required for the work. The extremely polarised atmosphere at the workplace is obvious from the facts which came to light after the bomb blasts in Mumbai and Delhi, wherein people lost their jobs because they were Muslims.

Table No. 4

	Do you work for a non Muslim employer?	*Is work affecting your prayer patterns*	*Preference to work in this area only*	*Feeling Muslim identity at work place*
A	–	–	4	7
B	6	3	2	7
C	0	2	9	6
D	13	4	4	4

Source: Field data

People who worked outside the area in places where people of other faiths also work, felt a sense of otherness, the sense of belonging to a community that involves itself in 'terrorist acts', which helped in constitution of their identity. One of our respondents, who joined an export house in Noida was suspected by his boss of being a terrorist. He used to remain silent in the office as he took time to adjust in a new environment. His boss, a graduate from IIM, suspected that he may be a terrorist, and was frightened. Some months later when the respondent became friendly with colleagues, he was told about this. Another respondent, originally from Azamgarh, used to live in Ashram with his brother. They were the only Muslims in the building and their landlord was a Hindu. He frequently hosted his friends, who happened to be Muslims carrying identifiable signs of their faith like beards, etc. His neighbours got suspicious and informed the police. The police raided their house but the landlord came to their rescue. He confirmed their innocence despite them being Muslims. Another respondent reported that he lost his job because of being a Muslim. A particular kind of Muslim identity, with its own attributes, was constructed by the violent act in Batla House. This identity did not only create polarisation between Muslims and non-Muslims but also generated a sense of fear within the

Muslims, resulting in removal of students and unmarried adults as tenants in the area around Jamia Millia Islamia. While no landlord wanted to become the next target of the State, it also compelled people to involuntarily acknowledge and become part of a larger discourse – that possibilities of terrorists being present everywhere should not be discounted and that everyone should be 'suspected' if he has particular attributes. It became the universe of discourse within which every other issue was dissolved and diluted, and every issue was understood within the framework provided by the incident.

It is the feeling of being an 'other' and being discriminated against that generally led the respondents to say that they would look for areas which are Muslim dominated, for settling down (Chart No.5).

Chart No. 5

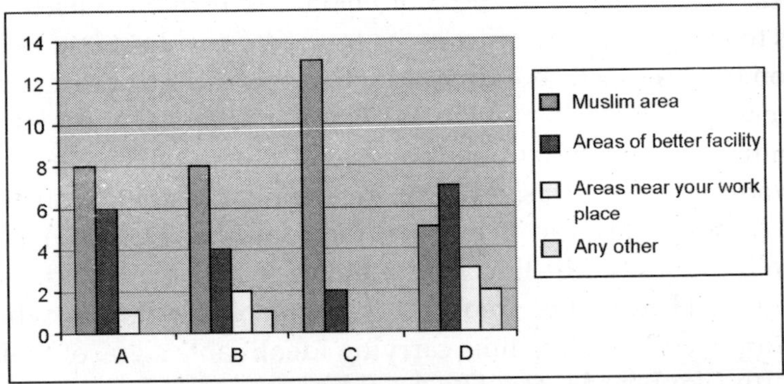

The development of Zakir Nagar provides us ample proof of the process by which the whole area became a Muslim dominated one from being one where mostly Hindu Yadavas and Gujjars lived. The process began in the 1970s and in around thirty years the demographic profile of the area has become one sided in terms of religious distribution. A number of people, apart from migrants from other states, shifted here from Old Delhi. Similar is the case of Abul Fazl Enclave, which started being settled in towards the end of the 1970s, when Mohammad Abul Fazl Farooqi, was inspired by a seminar held in Jamia Miilia Islamia in 1978, which unanimously decided "that there should be a colony where Muslims could establish their social and family life according to their own culture" (Farooqi, 2006, p. 53). The areas around Jamia Millia Islamia gradually developed into a full fledged ghetto, along with institutions; such as Markaz Jamaat-e-Islami Hind, Muslim Personal Law Board, the Islamic Fiqh Academy, the Institute of Objective Studies, Dr Zakir Husain Library and Museum, office of the Adalat Sharia Hazrat Nizammuddin Aulia, Maulana Abul Kalam Azad Islamic Awakening Centre etc. These have played an instrumental role in the consolidation of the collective identity.

The reason for the relocation of people was, as pointed by some of the respondents, that they were getting more land near the University. The area has often been often referred to as the 'graduate area', i.e. an area where learned people live. Some respondents said that they shifted here because they were hounded out of Hindu majority areas and also because culturally they could identify more closely with this place. Waqar narrated his shifting to the area in following words:

> "I had bought a piece of land in Karol Bagh. It is a mixed area, residential as well as commercial. The person next to my plot, Mishraji, when he got to know my Muslim identity in our first meeting, asked: *Yahan kya kar rahe ho*? (What are you doing in this area?) He said that I will not be able to live there and put up hurdles to evict me from there. My building (a commercial complex) was built and leased. The police would harass us. It was not that Mishraji had a lot of clout in the government, but being a government servant he knew how to write letters, as well as the procedures of follow up. It was the most stressful period of my life. I lost a lot of money and time. I still have my plot there but am not able to use it" (interview dated 2nd February 2009).

He shifted to this place though he could have stayed in other posh areas as well. His relatives stay in Nizammuddin East, which is an upscale colony. Though it is a Muslim dominated area, the Mosque is still far off, about 15-20 minutes walk from the house. Therefore, the *azaan* does not reach them. There is no culture of daily *namaaz* or *namaaz* circles there. He does not face similar problems here. When he is lax in his duties, he sees people going to the mosque and develops a sense of guilt. The *mahol* (environment) allows him to remain on the right track, and follow Islamic values and culture.

Another respondent said that he could afford to buy a place in a posh colony of South Delhi but would have lost his culture. He decided to shift from Old Delhi to this place because there are mosques in the vicinity and he gets persons who could teach the Quran to his children at home. One respondent, who works as a daily wage labourer (as a mason), said that he would get his kids admitted to the MMS (Milli Model School), a school run by a Muslim organization. His family looked after a *dargah* in his village. When he was told that in the school he mentioned he would learn a different Islam, that forbids these *mazar* matters, he replied, *"kuch tahzeeb to seekhega"* (they will at least learn some manners). At one level if this is about preserving the culture that one has inherited and accumulated over generations, whereas on the other it is about the nature of discomfort that one feels while away from a location that provided a person with a way of life that he considered appropriate and that in a highly polarised society that has become difficult. It is a certain form of alienation that one feels, being caught in the whirlpool of a religiously polarised society as well as a pang at the loss of one's culture and tradition (which can be easily critiqued by many as the effort to preserve the facets of a conservative ethos). Can there be a situation, for example, in colonies where one could go for his/her daily prayers? It is more than about accommodation of a different religion in one's time frame. It is about how we develop a discourse that relies on dialogic processes to minimise casualties and hatred, even in the long term.

We have seen above how identities are constituted. In this constitution of identities the state and other agencies such as the media, have not only further consolidated identities but have made them more vigilant about whatever goes on around them. The researchers were interrogated when they were taking pictures and many refused to respond to them. It is also because they are discriminated in their everyday life. Many of the respondents said that they were asked to provide their identity proof when they went to a cyber café in and around the area but when they went to New Friends Colony nobody stopped them. Different locations have different rules depending upon how state and its instruments view them. For instance, on 15th August and 26th January, Delhi Police puts up a metal detector on the road checking who all are leaving the area and with what.

Class and the Everyday Life

Identity formation has a definite economic dimension to it. It is the well-off section in the locality which is more concerned about its religious identity and tries to understand all its relationships with the outside world with reference to it. It is also so because it is the necessity of the elite to sustain itself in a hegemonic position. The poor on the other hand, for instance rickshaw pullers and the construction labourers, are least concerned about their Muslim identity. As the study was undertaken in the aftermath of the Batla House episode, police repression was one of the most talked about issues. Rickshaw pullers and construction labourers said that they lived the violence of the police in their everyday life. One rickshaw puller said: *"ham yahan bas ke kya karenge, hame to wapas hi jana hai"* (What will we settle here for? We have to go back home). A huge chunk of rickshaw pullers come from

Malda in West Bengal. While the Hindus go to Gurgaon, the Muslims come and stay here. That is where their identitarianism stops. They do not follow puritan ways of life or go to *mazaars* and are not members of any Muslim organisation. The violence perpetrated by the police holds a completely meaning for them. It is not the violence that was experienced through the Batla House episode. They live it everyday. The Police often abducts some of them (because FIRs are not lodged for everyone held by them) and keeps them in the police station till the contractor or the rickshaw owner comes and gives some money to the police.

The awe and domination of the upper class over them is complete. The poor say "we are like mosquitoes in front of the 'rich' man. We carry no weight at all. He behaves with us as if we are not even human beings". They are far removed from the religio-political activities of the area. They say *'haemin in baatoon se kya matlab hai'* ("what do we have to do with such matters'). Even those who have more or less permanently migrated to Delhi because 'they do not have any land back home nor any hope of a job there', don't participate in the public programmes which are held in the area.

Violence, as is being pointed here, is of two kinds – both embedded in the everyday life of people. One form of violence is subtle, which affects the physicality of the person when they are picked up by the police and are kept in interrogation rooms without any notice by the state and which also affects the mental structure of a person on occasions when they are frisked, when their movements are monitored and their existence is under constant surveillance. This kind of violence targets the students, the well to do persons who do not necessarily have to think about how to manage their food the next day. Second form of violence targets those who are already fighting to survive, unsure of whether they would get work the next day. When Batla House happened, it bothered them (as reported by respondents) because they were not allowed to take their rickshaws there or could not go out to work. The daily wage labourers reported that they were locked up for some time, may be hours, or even days sometimes on a regular basis. Actually, new constructions are not allowed in the area. They are possible only by bribing the police (as we were told). If some building is being constructed, the police comes and takes the labourers to the lockup. Hundreds of labourers have been locked up at least once because of it. One respondent said that he has been taken to the lockup many a time. "*Kya karein hamen hi pakad kar le jaya jata hai. Phir malik ko phone kiya jata hai, woh police ko badi rakam de kar humen chhuda kar le jata hai*" (What can we do? They take us to the police lock up. Then the owner is called up, who pays the police a hefty amount to free us). But people seem unaware of these events. "*Han, aisa ho sakta hai*" (it may be possible), one grocery shopper said. Whoever we asked about this said that they were hearing of this for the first time, and that it might be possible. It is a reflection of the way in which discourses on violence are constructed and how the 'popular' imagination of violence is constructed. These acts of the police are not taken as 'violent' as other acts in the area are. This violence, which is routinised, is also ignored because it does not carry the rhetorical value that would mobilise the masses, because it would also fracture the illusion of a homogeneous community that is constructed, and would reveal the fissures along class lines within the community. Why would a person who thrives on a business, being a landlord or an owner of an illegal workshop or industry be bothered about the fate of these workers? Hence, quite obviously, these events are not quoted in the posters describing state driven discrimination against Okhla. No call for mobilisation against such acts of violence is made. Rather the posters see the ban on constructions as an act of discrimination. *One needs to understand, therefore, the character of mobilisational politics and the collective identity formation in the area. It is not a working class political mobilisation. Rather it is a movement that seeks to downplay any kind of class polaristion that exists so overtly within the community. And as indicated by studies showing how decline of trade unions led to the discontent of people getting used by the right wing formations in Gujarat the same analysis holds true for our site of study as well. It reveals how ghettos thriving on the idea of an undifferentiated collective have a favourable climate for the elite to prosper.*

In these circumstances, it is obvious that the seasonal labourers do not feel interested in making this place their home. They say that the prices of land are exorbitant and in the same price they can buy 10 times more land back home. The city doesn't attract them at all. They hate it and they are here just to earn money, for which they tolerate the harsh treatment by the locals and stay in harsh conditions. It is because of the distinct class positions that one finds difference in the position of different segments regarding the issues that become symbols for the area. The poor condemn the Batla House incident because as a result of it they were not allowed to take rickshaws into those areas and an enormous number of policemen were placed there. Most respondents from lower classes are not "aware" of the political processes and interest based motives involve in the case. They do not have the fears that other people in the area have. "*Hamara riksha le jane nahi diya gaya,*" (we were not allowed to take our rickshaws), one respondent told us.

They don't narrate the Batla House incidents as vividly as students, corporate or the elite respondents. The rich take for granted that the lower class supports the idea of unity; they feel that everyone in the Muslim community is vulnerable in these times of the 'discourse of branding Muslims as terrorists'. For someone like Ehsaan, a construction worker, there was no fear when the Batla House incident happened. He says, "why will I fear? Why would police pick me? What have I done?" Students and people working in the corporate sector were quite scared that any one may be picked up or shot any time; there also was not a lot of fear of the police in the people who are politically active working as leaders of the community. One respondent said, "*police hame nahi pakad sakti. Ham to yahin ghumte hain*" (The police cannot pick us up. We are always around). The instruments of solidifying the idea of 'one community' don't work uniformly across classes.

State, Control and Identity

The state presents itself through the police in this area. Two police posts exist on the two main leading roads to the area symbolically indicating that they are guarding the entrance. Both the rich as well as the poor have been equally harassed and victimised by the police. The area a lot of illegal constructions, and the land mafia wants a free hand in their activity. However, the police has always sought bribes from them to allow new construction projects. For the poor, as narrated above, the police has been a routinised perpetrator of violence as it has been in relation to the youth of the area.[19] It is seen as an agency of the state which constantly looks for an opportunity to interfere in the day to day activities of the people. There is a section of the population (and certainly not the poor masses) which believes that the police is always on the look out for somebody as part of the state's hidden policy for Muslims. This argument may arise from the kind of fear that the police generates but it also becomes useful in

---

19. I remember how classrooms became empty after the Batla house episode. The fear of being picked up by the police and never to come back always haunted them. In a group discussion students revealed how all of them would huddle in the night at the sound of a police siren during those days.

mobilising people along a common identity that is repressed and under constant vigil.

What is interesting is that the routinised violence against the poor never becomes a news item whereas any act of the police which involves the elite of the area becomes the headlines. This routinised violence emerges, no doubt, as part of the ideological state apparatus but there is no semblance of resistance against it and that is what is surprising for an observer. The meaning and structure of violence, therefore, in the psyche also only relates to the repression of a particular kind – the one which can be portrayed as one against the community (and the violence against poor is not against the community!!). In other words, the principle of generalisation is used to represent the discrimination and victimhood of the whole community. The cases of violence that is faced by the rickshaw pullers or the construction workers would not contribute to formation of a collective identity that seeks to represent the interests of the Muslim elite. It would become a subversive agent. Therefore, it more that apparent that the public sphere appears biased and serving the interests of a few.

A similar act of physically hurting someone acquires different meanings in terms of 'violence'. While it directly affects all of them who suffer because of it, directly or indirectly, it treats one instance of hurting as more serious compared to the other (for instance that inflicts on rickshaw pullers or the construction workers). *An act of violence perpetrated by instrument of state is an aggression not only on the physicality of the individual but also on its territoriality – the spheres within which it moves for existence. It becomes an issue of the community at one instance and not on the other because internal polarisation and strife is never allowed to sharpen.* In both cases it interrupts the everyday life of people. But this interruption will have different meanings. For one (the rickshaw puller) the closing of the whole area for days meant a problem of survival, whereas for the elite the closing down becomes a symbol of repression and an opportunity for uniting the differentiated community. This is not a denial of the condemnation that should emerge against the acts of the police force at Batla House, and it would neither imply that the violence of the kind that it represented is an act of aggression on the basic right of everybody to have a fair trial. Locals (through a constructed sense of a united neighbourhood) saw this act of the state violence an act against the common people.

Policepersons, generally seen as ensurers of safety and security, entered in the area with guns in hand and interrupted everyday life. Shops were closed down. People locked themselves indoors. Not only did they shoot two young men but also opened fire in the air (as narrated by the witnesses) and generated a sense of fear. Violence inherently has the capacity to generate force, a force that breaks and redefines the context. The life of the people around the area changed drastically after the act. When moving around Batla House after the incident we were talking to people about how the environment of tension can be eased. A regular response we got was: *kuch nahin ho sakta; muslamano ko to marenge hi* (Nothing can be done; Muslims will be killed). It was a perceptive statement about the insecurity that they experience, and the suspicion with which they see the instruments of state. In everyday existence religion becomes the most identifiable entity, an identity which is constructed around the idea of discrimination and a constant threat of extermination. It becomes so intrinsic to the existence of the self that "it's not now the question whether you follow religion or not... Religion will follow you..." commented a respondent. People were followed by their religious identity. They were questioned about this identity wherever they went – at workplaces, in market place, as persons seeking accommodation on rent.

The identity question did not become important only outside the area. The frightened people reacted violently inside. A huge number of students who used to stay in the locality on lost their accommodation. One respondent rented a flat with two more friends, one of whom was Hindu, just a few months before the 'event'. There were 19 flats in the building. They were the only students living there. The other families living there were frightened by the event. They thought that having students in the building makes them vulnerable to the police, as they were killing students in false encounters. Having Muslim students amidst them made them very insecure. Hence, these families pressurised the landlord and the students to vacate the flat. Some students of the university had to change houses twice or even thrice in the year, being told that having students as tenants was not safe. This reflects the nature of suspicion and fear that is part of everyday existence in the area.

Chapter 7

Collective Identity and the Class Politics – Beyond the *Appearances* in a Ghetto

Fear and suspicion creates a collective identity. It is established through the ideological apparatuses that construct knowledge and perception. This knowledge and perception shows how particular forms of violence are essentially violence against the Muslim community, which is understood as a community that is undifferentiated, where principles of inequality do not hold and where the productions relations, from which actually all *apparent* realities emerge, do not reproduce an unequal system. Because of such a conceptualisation of collective identity working class interests are put on the backburner and it is the class interest of those who need to enhance their bargaining power in the market outside this ghetto which decides the agenda of the collective identity mobilisation. Identities, which are in a constant state of flux have internal dynamics of their own which is grounded in history. The collective identities, while establishing the agenda of marginality, repression and discrimination bring out the contradictions of a system, end up being instruments for the *nuevo* elite to establish itself and sustain its hegemony, and enter into the competitive logic of capitalism. This elite does not allow class distinctions and polarisations to surface as these would endanger its agenda and existence. If one obfuscates successfully the existence of class, that is so intrinsic to local society, it would allow the elite to continue with repressive, extra-coercive forms of surplus accumulation without any opposition. If the informalised labouring masses challenge and raise questions, which they are not raising now (as revealed by the fieldwork), about the nature of violence that they experience in their everyday lives, at the hands of the police as well as those of the elite Muslims at their workplace it would result in a class war, which the elite, so dexterously, has been trying to keep in abeyance.

The violence at the hands of the instruments of state, or the case of profiling of Muslims in India makes the issue a little more complex, but this complexity would unravel itself towards a resolution only if the class alliances between the working class cutting across religions is established. In the larger metanarrative of capital conflict between the Hindu and Muslim elite do happen over control over capital and power sharing, but they also engage in alliances whenever needed. How would one explain the Indian private capital owned by a non-Muslim entering into alliance with the local private capital in Muslim countries? Does it refuse to become a partner in reconstruction processes in Afghanistan or Iraq? It does not. As and when needed capital, when it comes to surplus accumulation, transcends all borders and differences. And if the process of capital accumulation can be facilitated through making use of differences, polarisations and boundaries, it does not mind keeping those differences alive. What needs to be understood and deciphered, in a certain sense, is the process/es of capital accumulation taking place through identitarian conclaves. It brings us to, then, the important characteristic of capital – that of competition, through which capital expands and sustains itself. This competition can be read into the very logic of identitarianism, not discounting the significance of other non-economic factors playing an important role in identity formation.

Hence, capital works on the logic of competition whereas

labour can effectively resist the hegemony of capital through the logic of cooperation. The process of ghettoisation hampers this cooperation. It breaks the possibility of unity across religion and caste because the dominant political paradigm constructs the community as homogeneous. Class is not the issue, as indicated by interviews with leaders who are striving to establish a political forum for Muslims or the ideologies inscribed and conveyed by the posters. The violence of the state needs to be problematised, but ghettoisation is not the answer to it. The answer lies in the process of politicisation, a process that would initiate mobilisation at all levels, questioning the nature of the state, participation of the community's elite in the state and addressing the marginalised interests of the poor. The problem begins at the stage of conceptualising the problem – communalism is seen as a conflict between two or more religions, the post independence state is seen as 'secular' and the Constitution as unproblematic. What lies beneath these concepts needs to be unravelled. Because they are seen neither as products of the system that we inhabit, nor as modes of reproducing the system, the answer, usually, accepted is along the lines of carving a 'personal' space that is deemed unproblematic. The space that we inhabit is a product of a variety of elements which interact with each other to produce and reproduce the *status quo* of the space. These elements are hierarchically placed with the ruling element (class) always trying to keep its hegemony intact. Unless this is broken through modes of mobilisation that would create a counter narrative to the existing modes of thoughts and perceptions, it would be difficult to destroy tendencies within as well as outside the ghetto that generate the need for illusory exclusive spaces in the first place.

References

Ahmad, Aijaz (1996) *Lineages of the Present: Political Essays*, Tulika: New Delhi

Ahmad, Imtiaz (ed) (1973) *Caste and Social Stratification among the Muslims*, Manohar: Delhi

Al-Azmeh, Aziz (2003) 'Postmodern obscurantism and the 'Muslim Question'', in Panitch, Leo and Leys, Colin (eds.) *Socialist Register 2003: Fighting Identities: Race, Religion and Ethno-Nationalism*, K P Bagchi & Company: Kolkata, pp. 34-60

Álvarez-Rivadulla M J (2007) 'Golden ghettos: gated communities and class residential segregation in Montevideo, Uruguay', *Environment and Planning*, Vol. 39, No. 1, pp. 47 – 63

Anwar, Ali (2001) *Masawat ki Jung: Pasemanzar: Bihar ka Pasmanda Musalman* (in Hindi),Vani Prakashan: New Delhi

Baldwin, Davarian L (2004) 'Black Belts and Ivory Towers: The Place of Race in U.S. Social Thought, 1892-1948', *Critical Sociology*, Volume 30, issue 2, pp. 397-450

Bhatty, Zarina (1996) 'Social Stratification Among Muslims in India', in M N Srinivas (ed) *Caste: Its Twentieth Century Avatar*, Viking, Penguin Books: Delhi, pp. 249–253

Brass, Paul R (October 30, 2004) 'Development of an Institutionalised Riot System in Meerut City, 1961 to 1982', *Economic and Political Weekly*, pp. 4839-4848

Brass, Paul R (23/08/2006) 'Organised riots & structured violence in India', *The Hindu*, available at http://www.thehindu.com/2006/08/23/stories/2006082307241000.htm, downloaded on 10th May 2009

Breman, Jan (April 20, 2002) 'Communal Upheaval as Resurgence of Social Darwinism', *Economic and Political Weekly*, Vol 37 No. 16, pp. 1485-1488

Breman, Jan (April 17, 1993) 'Anti-Muslim Pogrom in Surat', *Economic and Political Weekly*, pp. 737-740

Chandoke, Neera (2004) 'Re-presenting the Secular Agenda for India' in Hasan, Mushirul (ed) *Will Secular India Survive?*, Imprint One: New Delhi

Chakravarti, Anand (Oct. 12-18, 2002) 'Doubly Alienated Muslims: Some Implications of the Gujarat Carnage', *Economic and Political Weekly*, Vol. 37, No. 41, pp. 4246-4248

Chatterji, Roma and Mehta, Deepak (2007) *Living With Violence: An Anthropology of Events and Everyday Life*, Oxford University Press: New Delhi

Engels, Frederick (1977) 'Engels to J. Bloch', September 21 (-22), 1890, *Selected Works, Volume 3*, Progress Publishers: Moscow

Etzioni, Amitai (Mar., 1959) 'The Ghetto-A Re-Evaluation', *Social Forces*, Vol. 37, No. 3, pp. 255-262

Farooqi, Mohammad Abul Fazl (2006) *Ups and Downs: An Autobiography*, Pharos Media and Publishing Pvt Ltd: Delhi

Gimenez, Martha E (2006) 'With a Little Class: A Critique of Identity Politics', *Ethnicities*, Vol. 6(3), pp. 423–439

Government of India (November, 2006) *Social, Economic and Educational Status of the Muslim Community of India*, Prime Minister's High Level Committee, Cabinet Secretariat, Government of India: Delhi

Gramsci, Antonio (2004) *Selections from the Prison Notebooks*, Orient Longman: Chennai

Gupta Dipankar (2002) 'Limits of Tolerance: Prospects of Secularism in India after Gujarat', *Economic and Political Weekly*, Vol. 37, No. 46 (Nov. 16-22), pp. 4615-4620

Gupta, Dipankar (1982) *Nativism in a Metropolis: The Shiv Sena in Bombay* Manohar Publications: New Delhi

Habib, Irfan, Khan, Iqtidar Alam, Singh, K P (Jun. 1976) 'Problems of the Muslim Minority in India', *Social Scientist*, Vol. 4, No. 11, pp. 67-72

Harvey, David (2000) *The Condition of Postmodernity: An Enquiry into the Origins of Cultural Change*, Blackwell: Cambridge

Hasan, Zoya (2009) *Politics of Inclusion: Castes, Minorities, and*

Affirmative Action, Oxford University Press: New Delhi

Hasan, Mushirul (2004) 'Introduction' in Hasan, Mushirul (ed) *Will Secular India Survive?*, Imprint One: New Delhi

Hirsch, Arnold R (1998, original 1960) *Making the Second Ghetto: Race and Housing in Chicago 1940-1960*, University of Chicago Press: Chicago

Jaffrelot, Christopher (1999) *The Hindu Nationalist Movement and Indian Politics, 1925 to the 1990s*, Penguin: New Delhi

Jahangirabad Media Institute, Action Aid and Indian Social Institute (2006), *National Study on Socio-Economic Condition of Muslims in India*, Indian Social Institute: New Delhi

Joshi, Shashi and Josh, Bhagwan (1992) *Struggle for Hegemony in India. Movement, Vol. II: 1934-41*, Sage: New Delhi

Kirmani, Nida (2007) *Questioning 'the Muslim Women': The Narration of Multiple Idenities in Zakir Nagar*, A Thesis Submitted to the University of Manchester for the Degree of PhD in the Faculty of Humanities, School of Social Sciences

Kumar, Ravi (May 1, 2004) 'Ideologies, Practices and Communal Fascism in India: Reinventing Spaces of Contest', *Mainstream*, Vol. XLII (19)

Kumar, Ravi (December 12, 2008) 'All in the name of fighting terrorism: Profiling, Repression and Consensus Creation', *Radical Notes*, available at http://radicalnotes.com/journal/2008/12/12/all-in-the-name-of-fighting-terrorism/ downloaded on December 15th 2008

Madan, T N (Nov., 1987) 'Secularism in Its Place', *The Journal of Asian Studies*, Vol. 46, No. 4 (Nov., 1987), pp. 747-759

Mander, Harsh (19/10/2008) The Real Travesty, *The Hindu*, available at http://www.thehindu.com/thehindu/mag/2008/10/19/stories/2008101950100300.htm, downloaded on 17th January 2009

Marx, Karl (1977, original 1859) *'Preface to A Contribution to the Critique of Political Economy', Selected Works, Volume I*, Progress Publishers: Moscow

McLaren, Peter and Jaramillo, Nathalia E (2007) 'Katrina and the Banshee's Wail: The Racialization of Class Exploitation', *Cultural Studies ? Critical Methodologies*, Vol. 7 No. 2, pp. 202-221

Mohl, Raymond A (March 2003) 'The Second Ghetto Thesis and The Power of History', *Journal of Urban History*, Vol. 29, No. 3, pp. 243-256

Mukherjee, Mridula (Oct. 15, 1988) 'Peasant Resistance and Peasant Consciousness in Colonial India: 'Subalterns' and Beyond', *Economic and Political Weekly*, Vol. 23, No. 42, pp. 2174-2185

National Sample Survey Organisation (NSSO) (September 2001) *Employment and Unemployment Situation among Religious Groups in India, 1999-2000*, Report No. 468(55/10/6), NSS 55th Round (July 1999 – June 2000), National Sample Survey Organisation, Ministry of Statistics & Programme Implementation, Government of India: Delhi

NDTV (June 01, 2008) *Muslims issue fatwa against terrorism*, http://www.ndtv.com/convergence/ndtv/mumbaiterrorstrike/Story.aspx?ID=NEWEN20080051622&type=News, downloaded on 10th February 2009

Pandey, Gyanendra (1990) *The Construction of Communalism in North India*, Oxford University Press: New Delhi

Pandey, Gyanendra (Sep. 6-12, 1997) 'Partition and Independence in Delhi: 1947-48', *Economic and Political Weekly*, Vol. 32, No. 36, pp. 2261-2272

Pandey, Gyanendra (2001) *Remembering Partition: Violence, Nationalism and History in India*, Cambridge University Press: Cambridge

Pantham, Thomas (Summer, 1997) 'Indian Secularism and Its Critics: Some Reflections', *The Review of Politics*, Vol. 59, No. 3, Non-Western Political Thought, pp. 523-540

Pearson, Kim (2003) *Ghetto*, available at http://kpearson.faculty.tcnj.edu/Dictionary/ghetto.htm, accessed on 10th January 2009

Renton, Dave (2007) *Fascism: Theory and Practice*, Aakar Books: Delhi

Renton, Dave (2001) *This Rough Game: Fascism and Anti-fascism*, Sutton Publishing: Gloucester

Robinson, Rowena (2005) *Tremors of Violence: Muslim Survivors of Ethnic Strife in Western India*, Sage: New Delhi

Saberwal, Satish (2004) Anxieties, Identities, Complexity, Reality in Hasan, Mushirul (ed) *Will Secular India Survive?*, Imprint One: New Delhi

Scatamburlo-D'Annibale, Valerie and McLaren, Peter (2003) 'The

Strategic Centrality of Class in the Politics of "Race" and "Difference"', *Cultural Studies <—>Critical Methodologies*, Vol. 3, No. 2, pp. 148-175

Seligman, Amanda Irene (March 2003) 'What Is The Second Ghetto?', *Journal of Urban History*, Vol. 29, No. 3, pp. 272-280

Seron, Carroll and Munger, Frank (1996), 'Law and Inequality: Race, Gender...and, of Course, Class', *Annual Review of Sociology*, Vol. 22, pp. 187-212

Sonalkar, Sudhir, (June 26, 1993) 'The 'Muslim' Problem: A Perspective', *Economic and Political Weekly*, Vol. 28, No. 26, pp. 1345-1349

Suhrud, Tridip (2002) 'No Room for Dialogue', *Economic and Political Weekly*, Vol. 37, No. 11, pp. 1011-12

The Hindu (Aug 30, 2007) *Muslims take out peace rally in Devarakonda*, http://www.hindu.com/2007/08/30/stories/2007083052950300.htm, accessed on 12th Feb 2009

The Tribune (December 8, 2008) *Muslims take out peace march against terrorism*, http://www.tribuneindia.com/2008/20081208/delhi.htm#4, accessed on 12th January 2009

Ward, David (1982) 'The Ethnic Ghetto in the United States: Past and Present', *Transactions of the Institute of British Geographers*, New Series, Vol. 7, No. 3, pp. 257-275

Warner, Jr., Sam Bass and Burke, Colin B. (Oct., 1969) 'Cultural Change and the Ghetto', *Journal of Contemporary History*, Vol. 4, No. 4, *The Great Depression*, pp. 173-187

Wirth, Louis (original 1928, 1956) *The Ghetto*, University of Chicago Press: Chicago

Wirth, Louis (July 1927) 'The Ghetto', *The American Journal of Sociology*, Vol. 33, No. 1, pp. 57-71

Appendix

Qasim Rasool Illyas, a member of Jamaat-e-islami Hind's central advisory council, editor of a monthly called 'Afkaar' in Urdu and a prominent Muslim political activist, in conversation with Faisal and Sayeed. Illyas is also associated with dozens of Muslim organisations including All India Muslim Personal Law Board.

Faisal: The experience of last 60 years in politics shows that the secular parties have used us. The Muslim leadership has failed. What do you think the alternative could be?

Qasim Rasool Illyas: The first thing one has to understand is that in spite of the attitude of secular political parties, who don't address Muslim issues, Jamaat and other Muslim religious political organizations feel that the fascist and communal forces still pose a real danger. Secular parties make promises only to grab Muslim votes.

Despite such a situation because there is no alternative to the Congress in a lot of states, Muslims are forced to go with the Congress.

Second, whenever Muslims have got an alternative to the Congress they have preferred it. For example, the decline of the Congress in U.P is due to Muslims deserting it. SP has been relying on the Muslim-Yadav combination and Lalu in Bihar has had same arithmetic. They used to get 29-30% votes. This is 60% Yadavs and 30% Muslims and 5-6% some other social categories. But even these parties have not helped the

Muslims. But what is clear is that whenever Muslims have got an alternative they have encashed it.

And whenever Muslims have got a chance to make their own candidate contest they have gone for it. In Malegaon (Maharashtra) Muslims put forth their candidate and he emerged the highest vote gainer but because he couldn't get majority he had to take support of the Congress to become Mayor of the Corporation. The same happened in Assam where Muslims are in substantial numbers. So in a lot of constituencies Muslims had sufficient votes on their own to win elections whereas and in a lot more others their vote is crucial for deciding who would win. It was our (Jamaat) own idea. With an effort of just six months they were able to win 10 seats and lost 12 by only meagre margins. They were angry with the Congress as they had the will to launch the party.

So whenever they have been disheartened and dejected because of the secular party if they have got a secular alternative they have gone for it. In Bengal Muslims are not happy with the Left parties. So you will see the new combination of Mamta and Congress will garner Muslim votes and Left parties will suffer. The Left has ruled there for 30 years and the Sachar Committee report says that Muslims are in the worst situation there compared to any other state.

So Muslims are shifting to other secular alternatives, or any one who has talked about social justice. This happened in UP - when Muslims were not happy with Mulayam, they went with Mayawați. She got some other people in the name of social engineering; hence she came in a position to form a government. In UP, the Muslims are angry with Mulayam due to the inclusion of Kalyan Singh. They are angry with Mayawati for whatever she has done in the name of terrorism and the Congress is not in a position to get a good number. So this is causing Muslims to support either the existing, or newly formed Muslim political parties. Whether this support would make them win seats is not, it is too early to say. On the surface it doesn't seem it would make them win. Muslim votes will be divided and it could benefit or cause problems to the Muslims themselves. For example, Ayyub's party, Akhlaq Saab's party and the Ulema council are attracting huge crowds but will these crowds, translate into votes? We are not sure... Unless the Muslim leadership takes a clear line and is successful in communicating it, it can't bring out fruitful results and translate these crowds into votes. Now there are 6-7 organisations that have jumped into the political foray.

Jamaat's policy has been to support any strong contestant against the BJP. But for a change, in Kerala we openly supported LDF against UDF. In the Muslim pockets the Congress couldn't win a single seat. Out of Muslim League's 19 sitting MLA's only 7 could win. The reasons for the Muslims are very clear - they change according to their needs. But they don't support anyone at the cost of the BJP or any other fascist power's victory.

Another problem is evident apart from political parties ditching the Muslim community. Muslims too have not been successful in pursuing their agenda after the parties whom they have supported have won. They don't exert pressure on them. No lobbies work; we don't do our homework and do not guide our MP's and MLAs. Wherever there has been any effort it has borne results. For example, on the issue of Waqfs, the Muslim Personal Law Board had a marathon meeting and it made suggestions to improve the performance of Waqf. Now the Joint Parliamentry Committee has come out with suggestions which have largely been framed on the lines we had suggested.

When the Sachar committee was formed it interacted with Muslim religious and community organizations. We (Jamaat) had three meetings with them. A joint meeting with other Muslim organizations was held. And wherever it went (other states) we sent our local delegates to meet it. This interaction has helped a lot in bringing out a truer picture of Muslims. They have represented the Muslim psyche, what we think in various issues etc. All these were incorporated. There were facts and figures already but the interactions helped a lot.

A big problem with Muslims is that their's is defensive mentality. We make demands at the time of elections and don't pursue them at all after that. Even when we build pressure we don't put up a united show. Different parties go and meet the Muslim community and leadership at different points of times. The same thing happens with other communities a well but the advantage of other communities is that their people in those parties serve their interests.

All political parties represent one or the other section, which is their social base. Apart from three national parties - Congress, BJP and Left - all the regional parties serve regional interests. RJD, BSP, SP and others basically serve their own social constituency. The problem with Muslims is that they don't have a political party which is part of any alliance and serves them. The problem is that all the Muslim MPs and MLAs are part of one or another political party which serves its own social base. It may be RJD for Yadavs, BSP for Dalits or SP again for Yadavs. Muslims in those parties are just decorative pieces. If Muslims try to raise their voices for something which goes against the party's interest, they are silenced. For example, MP Ilyas Azmi and another from BSP raised the Batla House issue in Parliament by wearing Arabic scarves. Consequently, the party denied them tickets. Thereafter, the news has been that Ilyas Azmi has some how, by pressure and threat, been successful in getting a ticket but the other person hasn't got one.

As far as our experience with Congress is concerned, the Muslim MPs of Congress say that they haven't won on our support, they have got the secular vote. And, therefore, say that they cannot only represent us. That's why Muslims have also started feeling that we too should have a politics of our own. The vote is quite fragmented now.

All the Muslim MPs in different parties come from Muslim majority areas. That means Muslims support them if they are dissatisfied and if they do not vote, these people wouldn't win. Now the Muslim MPs have started to realise this. Some days back, the Muslim MPs across political parties met the PM on the issue of terrorism and presented a memorandum that Muslims were being targeted in India and also proposed that, on the lines of Malaysia, an investment firm should be established for the purpose of Haj affairs. But even today their voice is very subdued in the national parties and the party leadership exerts huge influence on them.

In Lalu's party, Mulayam and Mayawati's it's the same. Those Muslims are selected who may not be able to put in front Muslim issues forcefully. These parties unlike the Congress or the Left Parties are built on personalities. It is a one man show, one man rules. In The Congress and the Left now people have started to raise their voice.

Muslim organisations like Indian Union Muslim League and Ittehadul Muslimeen are very small at all India level. They can't play an effective role though they represent the Muslim social base. They have tried to serve where they are. The Indian Union Muslim League, when it was in power in Kerala, served Muslim interest quite a lot.

Even after 60 years of independence, why should we be dependent on other parties? We should have a party whose social base is among Muslims. But it should serve everyone's interests. According to our experience there is not even a single party which serves all the people of the nation.

Lalu and Mulayam serve Yadavas, BSP Dalits, and the Congress, the BJP even the Left serve the upper castes in this country. Only a party formed by the Muslims can serve everyone irrespective of all differences. We want a party which should be Islamic, secular and constitution abiding. It should be from the Muslims, but for everyone and should think for everyone. That's why the Jamaat has finally decided to form a political party. Islam and Muslim interests will be our main focus. But in a country like India we can't jump at once. We will try to serve our interest gradually. It would be better to change the system from within. It would be a secular party which will address the whole nation and the humanity at large.

This is what has happened in Turkey. Turkey's secularism is more stringent than India's. India's secularism is not against religion. It does not just give religious freedom but promotes religion. Turkey's secularism condemns religion and condemns every effort at religious propagation. But the Islamic movement there has stayed inside the constitutional framework and has gradually tried to change it. This is how Hamas (in Palestine) did. Not one changed the system, neither raised slogans to change it.

The Islamic movement by serving humanity, can bring the good souls of the country close to us. This is how it happened with a lot of Islamic movements. So, we need to launch a Muslim party which addresses the whole humanity of the nation. The party should be ours, control should be ours, but it should serve everyone. All the marginalised and deprived sections should be cared for and no injustice should be meted out to any one. This would stop disoriented ness of Muslim politics. Till we stand with a begging bowl in front of other political parties our problem will not be solved. We want to share Power not to seek from the Power. Tomorrow we should try to get power. How will that happen? Time will tell. But we need to start now.

Faisal: Movements like the Pasmanda Movement, and other Backward caste voice among Muslims say that the politics in the name of Muslims is only upper caste politics. It takes away all the benefits of reservation and other concessions. So, the idea of single Muslim identity should be challenged and the lower caste should be represented.

Qasim Rasool Illyas: there is more propaganda in this and less of reality. Look into the Mandal Commission report, for example, the so called backward caste among the Muslims have got reservations. I am saying "so called" because there is no caste system in Islam. But there are differences among us in the name of 'Biradari' and they are based on professions. Though slogans like Ashraf and Arzal were given but the basic difference is of profession. No profession in Islam is high or low. Amongst us the lower caste are socially and economically backward, Mandal has recognized these 'Biradaris'. So wherever Muslims have got reservation these 'Biradaris' are the real beneficiaries. Even the 4% reservation in AP also gives the benefit to these biradaris. We wanted the economic criteria to be followed in giving reservation to the Muslims but it was rejected by the Mandal Commission and in Andhra Pradesh. Now it is given on basis of social disadvantage to lower castes. The demand for reservations that has now been made by Muslim organizations, asks for the Muslim community minus the creamy layer to be taken as backward. So the whole community should be given reservations. Like this all those *'Biradaris'(caste)* that are economically backward will come in the category. But there are some *biradaris* which are economically well to do but socially they are thought to be backward, e.g, Qureshi. In Delhi, they are one of the better off *biradaris* but if you give reservations only to backward castes then the Qureshi will also get it, though they are economically well off.

Secondly, if you make 'biradaris' and castes the criteria for reservations you create a permanent cleavage in society. As far as the Hindu society is concerned this cleavage is present in the religion, so they don't have any problem with that. But where religion doesn't sanction it today or tomorrow these differences will dissolve. Why create those oppressive identities by reservation? Amongst us if there is a backward caste person, who is well off, economically, and educated, then there is no problem in him marrying outside his caste. For example, if a person stops keeping a Qureshi name and is economically well off, then there is no problem in his marriage etc. But if you keep the label and in that you see advantage of reservation, the so called social discrimination will continue. We have to address this issue and set criteria to decide what constitutes the 'creamy layer', and who should get reservations. In creamy layer category only those people will come who fall in the so called upper castes, and other economically well of castes would also come here. The majority who are discriminated against will get reservations.

Now, the Muslim organizations have come to a consensus in this after much debate. Three things seem to be very important:

1. Article 341 should benefit Muslim Dalits also. They shouldn't be discriminated against due to religion.
2. All the 'Bridaris' recognized by the Mandal Commission should be kept as they are.
3. The Muslim community should be taken as backward and excepting the creamy layer they should get reservation.

These are the demands. The recommendation by the Ranganathan Mishra report for 10% reservation for Muslims should also be extended. Whatever comes in Dalit quota should also be extended to the Muslim community. Only then would the discontent among the Muslims will be taken care of.

Faisal: But reservations may overlap...? A person is Muslim; he belongs to the Dalit category as well...

Qasim Rasool Illyas: No. A person can avail of reservation only in one category, whichever he wants to. General Muslims or dalit Muslim. In Mandal 27% backward Hindus are there. But the stronger among the backward are getting all the reservations. Just as in Andhra Pradesh where out of 27% reservation for OBC, 4% is for Muslims, elsewhere too Muslims should get a particular percentage. Once clubbed with the Yadavas they do not get it.. It is also our demand that under Mandal Muslims should get a specific percentage once you club them with Yadavs and others, they don't get it. On the lines of Karnataka, Muslims should be given a percentage in the Mandal category. Apart from all this the rest of the community should get 10%. Whoever among Muslims wants to take this, let them have it, which others may take it in their chosen category.

Sayeed: Do you think the issue of the Batla House encounter will be a major issue in the coming Lok Sabha election?

Qasim Rasool Illyas: The issue of Balta House will crop up during the elections somewhere or the other, like in Azamgarh and some other areas in UP. It is not dead. But it is basically an issue for UP and Delhi and may not go far. But the real issue is that of targeting of Muslims in the name of terrorism. This issue is present in almost all states. In some states like Maharashtra, Gujarat and Andhra Pradesh more atrocities have been committed than in others. In these states this issue dominates.

This has had an impact in Malegoan as I told you. In Aurangabad, Muslim Congress leaders resigned from Congress. But Maharashtra is very vast and there are only few pockets like Malegaon and Aurangabad. If all the Muslims in these constituencies come together they may win 4-5 seats in the state. But in other constituencies it is very difficult.

Faisal: One disturbing thing is that though the Jamaat's political party will address everyone, it seems that the Jamaat is depending largely on the Muslim constituency?

Qasim Rasool Illyas: Yes, Muslims are our social base. We have concentrated on them. But our approach is not communal. You (Jamaat cadre) shouldn't just be talking about Muslims you should try to solve everyone's problem. This is how politics gets played out. The example of the BSP is in front of us. They first consolidated the Dalit votes and then in the last elections they pitched candidates from others castes and communities. Thus, they made sure they got votes from both their and the candidate's social base. This is a model we can replicate, which has been successful for the BSP. If you are a Muslim or a Brahmin in the respective majority constituency and you can guarantee your community's vote then you get the seat. This has been called social engineering and has proved to be very successful. We want to consolidate the Muslim vote first. Then we can have non Muslim candidates getting their community's vote but serving us and them both. This seems to be a difficult job, but imposing it is all about how you manipulate.

Once our candidates get elected, he would work for all other communities as well. So the next time our candidate will be elected by other constituencies, also not just the Muslims.

Sayeed: Others have also made promises like these earlier. Why do you think people will believe you?

Qasim Rasool Illyas: Our aim is not to win Assembly and Parliamentary seats. Our aim is service. Please don't expect that we will fight on communal lines or only for the Muslim community. Even in selecting the candidates we will not give ticket to those who just want to be with us for power. We would not let character-less people contest with our ticket. Don't compare us with those political organizations whose aim is to capture power by hook or by crook. Even if we lose our ideology will be disseminated.

Sayeed: You mean you want to do things which others have promised but not delivered?

Qasim Rasool Illyas: More than that. They don't have any concept or ideology to back their claims. Communists do have that, but no one else. The Congress used to talk about socialism all those days but today it promotes capitalism. The inconsistency is due to lack of ideology. They have no political, social or economic ideology. That's why this is happening. For them social justice is to benefit their community whereas its true meaning is to give justice to very person in society.

This happens only when your policies are just. The present economic policy is unjust. That is why all problems are there. It is a country where 70% are in rural areas and largely dependent on agriculture but still a huge number of farmers commit suicide. It means something is wrong with your policy.

Faisal: How will you deal with the issue of police?

Qasim Rasool Illyas: The Supreme Court has itself stated that the police are goons in the uniform. It is a goon force. All the commissions setup to examine the police have given a very bad opinion about the force. But none of the recommendations are thought upon. The Police basically is a toy in the hands of the ruling political party. Investigations, and law and order should be separated. Now, the situation is that the police is the accuser, witness and the judge, plus the culprit a lot of times. This should be stopped.

Faisal: In Urban India, Muslim population gets concentrated in a particular locality, which affects their quality of life and as well as it affects their life in general. And then if politics is done focussing solely on Muslims as a social base will it not reinforce the problems emerging of their isolated physical location? Shouldn't there be an effort from inside the community not to concentrate like this to evade the danger at times of communal riots and lack of communication with larger community in normal times?

Qasim Rasool Illyas: There are problems: interactions cease and quality of life decreases. All good public schools are away from Muslim areas. The problem is of security in non-Muslim areas. But for a practicing Muslim it is difficult to retain one's Muslim identity by living in a non-Muslim area. Religious education of children in a non-Muslim area becomes difficult and non availability of mosques is also a major issue. Because of these a man slowly gets cut off from Islam. Here (in Muslim area) *Azaan* is heard regularly. This can't happen in a non Muslim area. It is not a small drawback but a huge loss. You can interview (Muslim) children from both areas (Muslim and non-Muslim) about their knowledge of Islam. You will know how much difference it makes among them as far as their Islamic identity is concerned. So, it is very important to stay in a Muslim area for the sake of identity. Apart from this Muslim colonies can be designed better, keeping in mind all necessities. The opportunity of interacting with the non-Muslim community in college, workplace etc, should be used. We (jamaat) think more about the rural areas than urban areas as we know more people are from rural areas. Their life is value based. Urban areas have money and media. Policy is made by the elite which is urban centric, though in number villages are more. That is why the Jamaat wants to start from the rural areas. We are not in a hurry. We don't plan to make it in 4-5 years. We will work slowly and solidly even if it takes 50 years. The Jamaat is the only Muslim organization which is all-inclusive among Muslims, sectarian differences are not important to us.

Faisal: what about the marginal status of women?

Qasim Rasool Illyas: We will give reservation to empower them; we have supported 33% reservation for women in Parliament. Even in the Jamaat, we have reserved one seat in every state. Anyways they can always get elected through the general quota.